Newfoundland Homestyle and Traditional Recipes

Copyright 1985
Second Printing 1987
Third Printing 1988 (Revised)
Fourth Printing 1989
Fifth Printing 1992
Sixth Printing 1995 (Revised)
Seventh Printing 1997

Table of Contents

Main Dishes

Nfld. Flipper Pie

(A Newfoundland Specialty)

Clean flippers and soak in boiling water and vinegar (½ cup warm water and 1 cup vinegar) for approximately 2 hours or overnight if desired. Rinse well. Make sure to remove as much excess fat as possible. Place in roaster.

Fry out salt pork (approximately 3 slices). Remove scrunchions and brown flippers in the fat. Add the following vegetables and cover with water

2 chopped onions
1 small chopped turnip
2 chopped carrots
1 chopped parsnip
5 or 6 chopped potatoes
salt & pepper to taste

Cover roaster and place in 350⁰ oven for 2 hours, adding more water if necessary. When done remove from oven and place pastry over top.

PASTRY

2 cups all purpose flour
2 tsp. baking powder
½ tsp. salt
½ cup shortening

Combine dry ingredients. Cut in shortening. Add enough water to make a stiff dough. Roll out to fit over flippers. Brush with milk. Place back in 375⁰ oven for approximately 15-20 minutes or until nicely browned.

Island Roast Partridge

Prepare 1-2 brace of partridge by soaking in vinegar water (1 tbsp. vinegar) for approx. ½ hour.

Pat dry. Sprinkle inside of birds with salt.

Stuff with savory dressing as follows.

DRESSING:

1½ cups dry bread crumbs
1½ tsp. savory
1½ tbsp. butter or margarine
1 small onion, chopped
Salt and pepper to taste

Place partridge in roasting pan. Put a slice of fat back pork or bacon over each bird.

Bake 325⁰F, covered or wrapped in foil for approx. 1½ hours, removing cover for last ½ hour to brown skin.

Island Baked Rabbit

1-2 brace of rabbits
fatback pork
flour and seasoning
vegetables

Skin and clean rabbits. Cut into sections. Dust with flour and seasonings. In large roasting pan fry out several rashers of pork and rabbit pieces, and brown well on both sides.

Cover with boiling water and place covered in 325°F oven for approximately 2 hours. Add desired vegetables during the last hour or so. Add more water if necessary.

About 15-20 minutes before serving, top with pastry. Increase oven temperature to 375°-400° and cook until golden brown.

Truly tasty!

PASTRY

2 cups all purpose flour
¼ lb. butter or margarine
½ cup cold water
2 tsp. baking powder
½ tsp. salt

Mix dry ingredients together. Cut in butter. Add water gradually, tossing with a fork. Roll out and cover rabbit and vegetables in roasting pan. Brush top with milk or egg white if you like.

Newfoundland's Own Figgy Duff

3¼ cups stale bread
1 cup raisins
½ cup brown sugar
dash salt
1 tsp. each allspice, ginger & cinnamon
¼ cup melted butter or margarine
¼ cup molasses
1 tsp. baking soda
1 tbsp. boiling water
½ cup plus 1 tbsp. all purpose flour

Soak the bread in water for about 10 minutes. Squeeze out excess water. Break into pieces and place in mixing bowl. Add raisins, brown sugar, salt and spices. Combine well.

Add melted butter, molasses and baking soda which has been dissolved completely in the boiling water.

Add flour and combine thoroughly.

Pour mixture into a dampened pudding bag and tie tightly leaving about ½ inch space between pudding and tie.

Boil gently for approximately 1½ hours.

Serve with "Lassy Sauce", (See recipe on page 47) or with traditional boiled dinner.

Newfie Jiggs Dinner with Peas Puddin'

2-3 lbs. salt beef
3 lg. potatoes (cut in halves)
1 medium turnip (cut in wedges)
2-3 lg. carrots (cut in halves)
1 head cabbage (cut in wedges)
1 pkg. split peas
pepper and salt
butter

Soak beef in cold water overnight. Throw off water. Cover with fresh water. Cook for approx. 2 hours, including peas pudding, as follows:

Place peas in dampened pudding bag or cloth. Tie securely. Place in with salt meat.

Approximately 30 minutes before meat is cooked, add vegetables, also remove peas pudding and mash with butter and seasonings. Retie and return for remainder of cooking time.

Dandelion

Dandelion is a common pest in anyone's garden, but can be turned into a nutritions dish. The leaves are dark green and spread in a rosette at the bottom. The flowers mature in to fluffy white balls. (Makes excellent wine!)

The young tender leaves are best. Later in the season they have a bitter taste and it is preferably to cook them in two waters.

Dandelion leaves or greens contain 25 times more vitamin A than tomato juice and 50 times more than asparagus.

The greens maybe eaten raw in a salad, mixed with an omelet, or cooked with a salt meat dinner (above).

Usually found in fields in early spring.

Turnip Tops

These tasty greens are usually served in the spring with salt-beef dinners.

3 lbs. fresh turnip greens (young tender tops)
2 tbsp. melted butter

Wash turnip greens and break off tough ends. Boil in salted water or salt-beef dinner. Serve with melted butter. Makes 6 servings.

Preparing Moose or Caribou

Moose meat is rich in flavor, lean, with a coarse texture, and can be cooked in the same way as stewing beef.

May be used as steaks, roasts, stew or soups. If using as steaks or roasts you may wish to marinate for approx. 24 hrs. before preparing. This ensures tenderness and flavour)

MARINATE **½ cup corn oil**
¼ cup white vinegar
⅔ tsp. salt
1 tbsp. chopped parsley
dash garlic powder
sprinkle of oregano and thyme

Island Moose Stew

2-3 lbs. moose steak
2 large onions
1 medium turnip
2 large carrots
1 parsnip
fat back pork
salt & pepper to taste

Fry fat back pork in stew pot until all fat is rendered out. Season moose with salt and pepper. Cut meat in cubes and brown well, with onion. Cover with water and simmer until tender (1½-2 hours). Add cubed vegetables. Cook until tender.

Cover with pastry (recipe follows):

2 cups all purpose flour
3 tsp. baking powder
1 tsp. sugar
¼ tsp. salt
shake parsley flakes
2 tbsp. butter or margarine
milk

Place dry ingredients in large bowl. Blend in butter. Add just enough milk to form soft ball.

Pinch off small pieces of dough and shape into patties.

Arrange on top of boiling stew. Cover tightly and cook approx. 10-12 minutes. Thicken stew just before serving.

Moose á la King

small moose roast (preferably frozen)
2 large onions (chopped)
salt and pepper to taste

Cut moose meat in very thin slices. Place in heavy skillet along with onions and brown in butter or cooking oil. Add seasonings. Cover and simmer on medium heat for approx. 15-20 minutes. Add little water if necessary. Thicken for gravy if desired.

Nice served on bed of rice. Accompanied with hot rolls and tossed salad.

Ruby's Chop Suey

2 lbs. moose meat cut in small pieces (or stew meat)
2 tsp. corn oil
2 cups water
2 chicken boullion cubes
1 tin mushrooms & juice
1 tin bean sprouts (drain & rinse in cold water)
1 green pepper-chopped
1 stalk of celery chopped
1 onion chopped
4 tsp. soya sauce
2 tsp Worchestershire sauce
½ tsp. M.S.G.
salt and pepper to taste
2 tbsp. cornstarch in
3 tbsp. water (for thickening)

Heat oil in fry pan. Add onion and brown meat. Transfer to large saucepan and add water, chicken cubes and juice from mushrooms. Cook until tender. Add vegetables, soya sauce, Worchestershire sauce, M.S.G., salt and pepper to taste. Cook until vegetables are tender, then thicken with cornstarch mixture.

Serve on a bed of cooked rice.

Marie's Salt Beef Stew

1-2 lbs. salt beef (cut in cubes)
1 cup carrot
1 cup turnip
½ cup parsnip
1 medium onion

Place salt beef in a large pot. Cover with approx. 2 quarts of water. Boil for approx. 1 hour. Remove 2-3 cups of the water and replace with fresh boiling water. Add cubed vegetables and sliced onion.

Continue cooking for another half an hour or until vegetables are tender.

Serve with hot rolls or homemade bread.

St. John's Style Crispy Potato Skins

(Nice snack while watching T.V.!)

6-8 baked potatoes
parmesan cheese
bacon bits
garlic powder (optional)
melted margarine

Cut potatoes in quarters lengthwise. Scoop out some of the potato and lay aside for later use.

Place potatoes on baking sheet, brush with melted margarine. Top with garlic powder, bacon bits and parmesan cheese.

Place in hot oven, 375-400ºF for approx. 15 minutes or pop under broiler until crispy and brown.

Truly delicious.

Clarenville's Classic Sandwich Loaf

1 loaf unsliced sandwich bread (preferably 1 day old)
soft butter or margarine
2 - 8 oz. pkgs. soft cream cheese
3-4 tbsp. light cream
chopped parsley, lettuce, tomatoes - for garnish.
choice of fillings (below)

With sharp knife trim all crusts from unsliced sandwich loaf. Turn on side and cut horizontally into four equal slices. Butter lightly both sides of layers except for top and bottom.

Place bottom slice buttered side up, on waxed paper, covered board or cookie sheet. Spread to the edges with chosen filling. Place second layer or slice on top of this and cover with second desired filling.

Add third slice and spread with third filling. Top with fourth slice (unbuttered side up). Gently shape loaf so that sides are even.

Remove any excess filling.

TO ICE: Whip cheese with enough cream to make it light and fluffy and easy to spread. Cover top and sides of loaf. Sprinkle with parsley if desired. Chill for 2-3 hours before serving.

When ready to serve place sandwich loaf gently onto a decorative tray or platter. Surround with lettuce leaves, cherry or sliced tomatoes, cucumber slices or whatever you so desire.

Slce loaf into 1'' slices (Usually makes 8-10 slices.

FILLINGS:

Crab Meat Filling

1 can crab meat (6 oz) drained
mayonnaise to taste
dash lemon juice. Mix together.

Egg Salad Filling

3 hard cooked eggs
2 tbsp. chopped olives
1 tbsp. chopped green onion. Combine.

Ham and Cucumber Filling

4 or 5 slices lean ham
1 cucumber (seedless, thinly sliced)

Nippy Cheese Spread

½ lb. process cheese
2 tbsp. catsup
1 tsp. worcestershire sauce
Cream cheese and blend in remaining ingredients.

Use any three of the above four fillings in sandwich loaf or substitute for your own favourite filling.

Nfld.'s Classic Beef Stroganoff

1 lb. beef sirloin cut in ¼" strips
1 tbsp. flour
½ tsp. salt
2 tbsp. margarine or butter
1 cup thinly sliced mushrooms
½ cup chopped onion
1 clove garlic
2 tbsps. butter or margarine
3 tbsps. flour
1 tbsp. tomato paste
1¼ cups beef stock or can condensed beef broth
1 cup dairy sour cream
2 tbsps. cooking sherry

Dust beef strips with the flour and salt. Heat skillet adding the 2 tbsps. butter. Brown meat quickly on all sides.

Add mushroom slices, onion and garlic. Cook for 3 or 4 minutes or until onion is tender. Remove meat and mushrooms.

Add 2 tbsps. butter to skillet drippings. When melted add 3 tbsps. flour. Add tomato paste. Now slowly pour in cold meat stock. cook and stir until thickened.

Return browned meat and mushrooms to pan. Sitr in sour cream and sherry. Heat briefly.

Keep warm over hot water.

Serve over a bed of rice or hot buttered noodles.

Yields: 5-6 servings.

Beef and Macaroni Casserole

½ pkg. macaroni noodles
¼ cup catsup
1 small tin tomatoes
2 large onions, chopped fine
1 lb. lean ground beef
1 tsp. salt
pepper to taste

Cook macaroni. Drain well. In a large hot frying pan with little oil, brown onions. Add ground beef. Cook well. Add remaining ingredients, stirring constantly. Cook gently for 10-15 minutes. Add macaroni. Combine well.

Transfer to casserole dish and serve hot with nice fresh dinner rolls and favourite salad.

Sandy's Mini Pizza

6 hamburger buns or English muffins
1 pkg. hamburger meat (cooked)
½ lb. or less grated mozzarella cheese
½ lb. cooked bacon (crumbled)
½ can mushrooms
1 small chopped green pepper
1 small diced onion
¼ tsp. garlic salt
1 tsp. oregano
dash pepper
1 can tomato sauce

Split and slightly toast buns or muffins.

Combine ingredients and mix with enough sauce to moisten.

Spread on buns and place on cookie sheet in preheated 350°F oven for 10-15 minutes.

Anne's Sukiyaki

¾ lb. boneless sirloin steak
meat tenderizer
3 tbsp. corn oil
1 medium onion, thinly sliced
½ cup thinly sliced celery
4 scallions or green onions, sliced lengthwise
4 large fresh mushrooms, sliced
¼ lb. fresh spinach, cleaned and corasely torn
1 tbsp. sugar
3 tbsp. soy sauce
1 cup beef bouillon

Sprinkle meat with meat tenderizer. Cut meat across the grain into very thin slices. Heat the oil in a skillet to almost smoking point. Add meat slices and brown quickly on all sides. Remove from skillet. Add onion, celery and scallions to skillet and cook 2 minutes, or until crisp-tender. Add mushrooms and cook 1 minute. Return meat to skillet. Add spinach. Sprinkle the sugar over top, then add soy sauce. Pour beef bouillon over spinach and stir gently to blend. Heat just until spinach wilts and mixture is piping hot. Serve immediately over hot rice. Serves 2.

Baked Bologna

1 small bologna (2 or 2½ lbs.)
1 tin of pineapple rings (15 or 19 oz.)

Drain pineapple and cut rings in half. Bring juice to boil, adding 2 tablespoons of brown sugar, 1 tablespoon of vinegar. Thicken with a bit of cornstarch. Line a loaf pan or a long dish with tin foil to cover this dish completely. Skin bologna and cut off a small slice lengthwise, so it will sit firmly in pan. Make slits 2 inches apart and 2 inches deep, about 8 slits in all. Insert pineapple half in each cut. Any leftover pineapple can be placed around sides. Three or 4 whole cloves for flavor. On top, pour the juice mixture over the bologna. Seal with tin foil and bake about 1 hour in a slow oven, 250°. This dish can be served with rice or vegetables.

Potato Logs

3 or 4 large potatoes
butter or margarine
2 eggs
corn oil
salt and pepper
parmesan cheese (optional)
bread crumbs

Boil potatoes. Drain and let dry. Mash with butter, 1 egg, salt and pepper. Let cool. Shape into logs or small one inch balls.

Coat each log in flour and dip in beaten egg. Roll in fine bread crumbs.

If desired shake some parmesan cheese in with the bread crumbs or mash with the potato, whichever your taste buds prefer. Place in deep fryer until golden brown.

Barbecue-Style Pork Chops

6 pork chops
1 tsp. salt
¼ tsp. pepper
1 tbsp. flour
2 tbsp. vinegar
¼ cup catsup
½ cup pineapple syrup
1 sm. chopped onion
1 med. green pepper
(cut in cubes)
5 slices pineapple (cubed)

Pre-heat heavy frying pan. Trim excess fat from chops. Combine flour and seasonings. Dip chops in this and place on skillet. Brown well on both sides. Combine vinegar, catsup, syrup, onion, green pepper and pineapple. Pour over chops. Cover and simmer for 45 minutes. If necessary, add more water.

Ralph's Beef Steak and Kidney Pie

1 lb. beef kidney
1½ lbs. round steak
1 large chopped onion
about 2 tbsp. corn oil
flour
salt and pepper to taste
3-4 cups hot water

Cover kidney with baking soda and water for about 1 hour. Rinse and remove the white membrane from kidney. Cut in slices. Also cut steak in small cubes.

Combine flour and seasonings. Dust meat with flour mixture.

Meanwhile heat a heavy skillet. Add corn oil, chopped onion and floured meat. Brown well on both sides. Add hot water. Cover and simmer for about 1½ to 2 hours. Transfer to large casserole dish and top with pastry, making slashes in top to let steam escape.

Place in 425°F oven for about 20-30 minutes or until pastry is golden brown.

Chili Con Carni

1 lb. ground beef
1 tbsp. corn oil
1 large chopped onion
1 tin tomato soup
1 sm. tin stewed tomatoes
1 tin kidney beans (14 oz.)
1 tsp. salt
dash cayenne pepper
2 tsp. chili powder
¼ tsp. oregano

Brown beef. Add onion and continue cooking until onion transparent. Drain fat. Add remaining ingredients. Simmer 30 minutes. Serve with rice and hot rolls.

Lasagne

1 lb. lean ground beef
1 garlic clove (minced) or garlic powder to taste
1 tsp. parsley flakes
1 tsp. oregano
1 med. onion (minced)
1 tsp. salt
1 cup tomatoes (optional)
1⅓ cups tomato paste
1 small tin sliced mushrooms
10 oz. lasagne noodles
1½-2 cups creamed cottage cheese
2 eggs (beaten)
1 tsp. salt
½ tsp. pepper
½ cup parmesan cheese
1 pkg. mozzarella cheese (approx. 6-8 slices)

In a heavy skillet brown meat. Spoon off fat. Add next eight ingredients. Combine well. Simmer uncovered for approx. 30 minutes (to blend in flavours), stirring occasionally. Meanwhile cook noodles until tender. Rinse in cold water. In small bowl combine cottage cheese, eggs, seasonings and parmesan cheese. Set aside. Lightly grease a large casserole dish (12''x7'' approx.) and beginning with noodles, alternate layers of meat sauce and cottage cheese and noodles. Top with the mozzeralla cheese slices. Sprinkle with a dash of paprika if you like.

Bake in 350° oven for 20-30 minutes. Let stand for 10-15 minutes before cutting.

Great served with crispy dinner rolls and tossed salad.

Paul's Spaghetti Sauce

1 lb. ground beef
1 med. onion (chopped)
1-2 stalks celery (chopped)
1 (14 oz. tin) spaghetti sauce
1 (10 oz. tin) cream of mushroom soup
1 cup tomatoes (chopped)
¼ ts. pepper
¼ tsp. salt
½ tbsp. chili powder
½ tsp. garlic powder
1 tsp. soya sauce
1 tsp. sugar

Brown meat in heavy skillet, along with onion celery, salt and pepper (over high heat). Remove from heat and add remaining ingredients. Return to pan and simmer covered for 1 hour. When ready serve over prepared spaghetti.

P.S. This sauce freezes well. When reheating warm it in oven — this avoids burning or sticking.

Traditional Porridge

(Nutritious breakfast cereal.)

1 cup rolled oats **3 cups water** **¾ tsp. salt**

Add salt to boiling water in saucepan.

Sprinkle in the dry rolled oats, stirring constantly.

When cereal begins to thicken, cook over low heat for 20 minutes. Stir several times during cooking. Add more water if necessary.

Serve with brown sugar, molasses and milk.

Newfie Style Baked Beans

2 cups dried white beans
¼ cup salt pork, diced
3 tbsp. brown sugar
1 tsp. salt
¼ cup molasses
½ tsp. dry mustard
1 medium onion, chopped
2 tbsp. catsup
dash worchestershire sauce
water

Wash beans thoroughly.

Soak beans in cold water overnight.

Place the beans and the water in which they were soaked in a pot and cook for half an hour.

Transfer to pot or pressure cooker.

Add the diced salt pork, brown sugar, salt, molasses, dry mustard, chopped onion, catsup and worchestershire sauce. Mix well.

If there is not enough liquid to cover the beans, add boiling water so the beans will be covered.

Cover bean pot and bake in a slow oven, 250ºF, for approximately six hours. Remove the cover from the bean pot during the last half hour of baking.

You may need to add some boiling water to the beans two or three times during the baking in order to keep the beans moist and covered with liquid. However, do not add any water during the last half hour of baking.

P.S. For a faster method, place all ingredients in pressure cooker and cook for 45 minutes.

Home Fries with a Difference

3 or 4 large baking potatoes
3-4 tsp. corn oil
salt to taste

Scrub potatoes. Do not peel. Cut with potato cutter or by hand to desired shape.

Brush all sides with oil. Place on shallow baking dish. Sprinkle with salt (optional) or desired seasoning.

Bake 350ºF for 30-35 minutes or until tender and golden brown.

Serve at once!

Tasty Marinated Steak Slices

vegetable oil
approx. 2 lbs. round steak (thinly sliced)
soya sauce
meat tenderizer
garlic powder
onion powder
vinegar

Slice meat into strips. Sprinkle with spices and tenderizer. Place in bowl and marinate with soya sauce and vinegar (approx. ⅔ & ⅓ or to suit your own taste).

Place in refrigerator for one hour (or longer if desired), turning now and then.

Fry quickly in oil at high temperature. Drain meat and enjoy.

Nice served on a bed of rice.

Oriental Meat Ball Casserole

(Elegantly delicious)

1½ lbs. gr. beef
2 eggs
2 tbsp. vegetable oil
¾ cup dry bread crumbs
2 oxo onion cubes
½ cup boiling water
½ tbsp. each salt, pepper
1-14 oz. can pineapple
dessert cubes
2 tbsp. cornstarch
½ cup brown sugar
3 oxo beef cubes
(or 4½ tsp. liquid)
1½ cup boiling water
½ cup white vinegar
¼ cup ketchup
¾ cup small sweet Gherkins
2 green peppers
cut in bit size pieces
2 carrots
cooked & diagonally
sliced

Combine beef, eggs, bread crumbs, onion cubes, dissolved in boiling water, salt and pepper. Shape into balls. Brown in 2 tbsp. oil. Drain. Drain pineapple, reserve juice.

Combine cornstarch, sugar and pineapple juice in sauce pan.

Add beef cubes dissolved in boiling water, vinegar and ketchup.

Cook, stirring constantly until thickened and bubbly.

Reduce heat, gently stir in meat balls, pineapple and remaining ingredients. Heat through, serve with rice or as an appetizer.

Makes 6-8 servings.

P.S. Great for pot luck suppers.

Baked Ham with Scalloped Potatoes

1 5-6 lb. ham
6-8 potatoes
salt and pepper to taste
boiling water
¼ cup butter or margarine
1 large onion (chopped)
2 cups milk
2 tbsp. brown sugar
2 tbsp. flour
enough corn syrup to
make a paste
1 tbsp. mustard
dash of paprika
cloves

Remove most of skin from ham. Place in a shallow roasting pan. Bake uncovered for about 2 hours. Remove from oven and make diamond shape cuts in fat. Place a clove in centre of each diamond.

Combine mustard and brown sugar. Spread over scored fat.

Meanwhile wash and peel potatoes. Slice about ¼ inch thick. Place in saucepan with salt and boiling water. Boil until potatoes are fork tender. Drain well.

In a separate saucepan melt butter or margarine. Add onion, sauté until golden brown. Add flour and seasonings. Gradually add milk stirring constantly over medium heat until it begins to thicken a little.

Place prepared potatoes around ham. Spoon sauce over potatoes. Sprinkle with paprika. Return to 375°F oven for approx. 45 minutes.

Honey Garlic Ribs

4 lbs. pork side or back ribs
½ cup chopped onion
2 cloves garlic, finely chopped
1½ cups ketchup
1 cup honey
2 tbsp. vinegar
2 tbsp. steak sauce
1 tsp. prepared mustard
½ tsp. salt
½ tsp. freshly ground pepper

Cut ribs into serving portions. Simmer in lightly salted water to cover for 30 minutes.

In saucepan, combine onion, garlic, ketchup, honey, vinegar, steak sauce, mustard, salt and pepper. Bring to boil and cook, stirring occasionally, for 5 minutes.

Drain ribs and place in shallow baking pan. Pour sauce over ribs and bake in 400ºF oven for 45 minutes or until tender and well glazed. Baste with sauce every 10 minutes. Makes 6 servings.

Barbecue Spare Ribs

3-4 lbs. fresh spare ribs
⅓ cup chopped onions
1 cup ketchup
⅓ cup worchestershire sauce
1 cup thick tomato sauce
1 tbsp. brown sugar
1 tsp. mustard
salt and pepper to taste
1½ - 2 cups water

Cut ribs in small serving pieces. Place in baking pan and cover with onions. Bake in 400° oven for about 30-40 minutes or until nicely browned.

Combine remaining ingredients and pour over ribs. Reduce heat to 350°, cover and bake another 40 minutes. Remove cover and baste. Continue baking for about another 15-20 minutes.

Nice served with rice and a tossed salad.

Pork Chops on Amber Rice

6 pork chops (¾'' thick)
salt and peper
1⅓ cups precooked rice
1 cup orange juice
1 (10½ oz.) can condensed chicken rice soup

Brown pork chops in heavy skillet. Season with salt and pepper. Place rice in 12 x 7½ x 2 inch baking dish. Pour orange juice over rice. Arrange browned pork chops on rice. Pour chicken soup over all. Cover and bake in moderate oven at 350º for 45 minutes. Uncover and bake 10 minutes longer. Makes 6 servings.

Crispy Chicken Fingers

4 or 5 large chicken breasts (skinned and boned)
2 large eggs
1½ cups stale bread crumbs
⅔ cup parmesan cheese
dash garlic powder if desired
½ cup margarine or more as needed

Cut chicken into strips (about 3 or 4'' in length and ½'' wide).

Dip into beaten eggs, then into mixture of bread crumbs, garlic powder and cheese.

Heat heavy fry pan and melt the butter. Cook chicken fingers until crisp.

Drain on paper towels. Serve at once.

"Finger lickin' good!"

Barbecued Chicken

1 large chicken (cut up)
1 cup flour
dash pepper
1 tsp. salt
½ cup cooking oil
½ cup chopped onions
1 tsp. vinegar
1 tsp. worcestershire sauce
½ tsp. chili powder
½ tsp. black pepper
½ cup catsup
½ cup cold water
2 tsp. paprika

Heat oil in large heavy skillet. Coat chicken pieces in flour mixture and place in oil on pan. Brown well on both sides. Make barbecue sauce from remaining ingredients, by placing in saucepan and simmering together for approximately 15 minutes. Next pour over browned chicken which has been placed in a large casserole dish. Bake in moderate oven 350ºF for approx. 30 minutes.

Honey Garlic Wings

3-4 lbs. chicken wings (discard tips)

Bake for 15-20 minutes in 400°F oven. Pour off fat. Meanwhile combine:

½ cup beef boullion
garlic powder to taste
¼ cup ketchup
¼ cup soya sauce
1 tbsp. vinegar
¼ cup brown sugar
¼ cup honey

Pour over wings. Cook in 350° oven for 1 hour covered.

Peppery Steak

1¼ lbs. round steak
2 tbsp. olive oil
2 tbsp. minced onion
1 clove crushed garlic
2 green peppers (sliced)
1 tin mushrooms
½ cup chopped celery
1 tsp. soya sauce
3 tbsp. cornstarch (mixed with 2 tbsps. water)
1 cup consommé

With a sharp knife, slice steak in thin diagonal slices. Heat large fry pan, add oil, onions, and steak. Brown well. Next add garlic, pepper, celery, plus one half cup of the consume. Add mushrooms. Cover pan. Reduce heat and cook for 15 minutes.

Add cornstarch and water to mixture, stirring vigorously. Add more consommé if needed to make a smooth sauce. Add soya sauce and simmer for another 5 minutes.

Serve at once on a bed of fluffy rice if desired.

Creamed Potatoes with a Difference

3-4 lbs. potatoes
¼ cup butter or margarine
½ cup cheddar cheese (grated)
1½ cups sour cream
salt & pepper to taste
2 green onions (chopped)
2 tbsp. margarine or butter

Peel potatoes and cook until tender. Drain and let dry. Mash with ¼ cup butter, sour cream, salt and pepper. Blend in half the cheese, beating until smooth. Stir in onions.

Pour into large greased baking dish or casserole. Smooth with a spoon dipped in milk. Dot with the remaining butter and sprinkle with remaining cheese.

Place in a pre-heated 350ºF oven for approx. 20-30 minutes. Then place under broiler for a few minutes to brown top.

Serve with your favourite meal.

P.S. This may be made ahead and kept in the refrigerator overnight.

Elegant Baked Liver

1½ lbs. liver
½ cup flour
1 tsp. salt
¼ tsp. pepper
2 tbsp. butter
1½ cups thick sour cream

Soak liver in boiling water 5 minutes. Roll in flour seasoned with salt and pepper. Melt butter in fry pan, brown liver on both sides. Place in greased baking dish. Blend 2 tbsp. flour with sour cream and pour over liver. Cover and bake in moderate oven, 350ºF, for 15 minutes. Remove cover and bake 25 minutes longer.

Serve with your favourite vegetables.

Traditional Fish Dishes

Tips!

Fish is so nutritious that it has often been called "brain food". It is found to be high in protein, the B vitamins, and many minerals. Salt water fish provides an excellent source of iodine. Fish is also a low-cholesterol food.

To keep fish white, add one tablespoon lemon juice and ½ tsp. salt to 1 quart of water used for boiling fish.

For a welcome improvement in flavor, sprinkle canned fish, such as salmon or tuna, with lemon juice before adding white sauce.

Trout must be kept clean, dry and cool (storing it in moss is good while in the woods). Frying trout in butter with freshly ground pepper is best. Remember they curl up when freshly cooked so tend them carefully.

Fresh fish should have firm flesh which springs back when dented with fingers. If fish is truly fresh, it should be odourless and free of slime; however, salt water fish will smell like the sea from which it came.

To thaw frozen fillets, place unopened package in the refrigerator overnight. Or, for quicker thawing, place unopened package in cold water **for 1 to 3 hours or in microwave for 3-5 minutes per lb.**

When cooking frozen fish, thaw in refrigerator (never at room temperature) in its original package for approximately six hours per pound. Use immediately after thawing or store in fridge up to 24 hours only. Never refreeze.

Most fish can be cooked while frozen. However when thawing is required, defrost fish in refrigerator or in microwave oven on defrost cycle.

Before cooking, rinse fish under cold running water to remove surface bacteria. Pat dry with paper towels to remove excessive moisture.

Do not overcook fish!

Overcooking makes fish tough, dry and tasteless. To prevent overcooking, test fish at the thickest part for doneness.

Done when fish turns opaque and flakes easily when tested with a fork.

Provincial Fish and Brewis

A Traditional Newfoundland Dish

2 lbs. salt cod
4 cakes of hard bread
salt pork (cut in cubes) about
1 cup (rendered out)

Cover fish and hard bread separately with cold water. Let soak overnight. Next day pour off water from fish and add fresh water. Bring to a boil. Boil gently for about 20 minutes. Remove from heat, drain and remove bones. Bring hard bread to a boil. Remove from heat and drain. Immediately add the cooked fish and the "scrunchions" (which are small pieces of fat pork rendered to a golden brown on a heavy skillet).

Serve at once "as is", or with molasses.

Some good b'y!

Baked Scallops Au Gratin

3 tbsp. butter or margarine
6 scallions, thinly sliced
½ lb. mushrooms, thinly sliced
3 tbsp. all-purpose flour
½ tsp. salt
¼ tsp. pepper
½ cup light cream
½ cup dry white wine
1½ lbs. scallops
2 tbsp. grated parmesan cheese

Preheat oven to 375°F. In medium skillet, melt butter over medium heat. Cook scallions and mushrooms 5 minutes, stirring often. Blend in flour and next two ingredients. Cook 1 minute. Add cream and wine. Cook, stirring, until thickened; do not boil. Place scallops in shallow baking dish. Top with sauce then sprinkle with cheese. Bake 30 minutes. May be placed in individual Ramkins or shells.

Hilda's Fish Stew

(Tasty)

1-2 lbs. fresh cod

Dust each side lightly with flour

Fry out some salt pork. Brown fish on one side.

Layer fish, onion rings, sliced potato (dusting each layer with flour) salt & pepper. Pour over this one cup water. Dot with butter. Let simmer until potatoes are tender, then add about ½ cup tin milk. Let heat through for a few minutes.

Enjoy

Fish Cakes, Carbonear Style

2 cups codfish, cooked and flaked (saltfish is best)
3 cups mashed potatoes
2 tsp. finely chopped onion
salt to taste (if fresh fish used)
1 egg

If salt codfish is used, soak overnight. Cover with fresh cold water and bring to boil for 20 minutes.

Flake the cooked fish.

Blend flaked fish, mashed potatoes, onion and egg together. Add salt if necessary, also sprinkle of savory.

Form into patties & dust with flour.

On hot frying pan, cook until golden brown on both sides.

Fried Cod Tongues

1 lb. fresh or frozen cod tongues
½ tsp. salt
¼ tsp. pepper
1 tsp. minced onion
6 slices fat back pork
1 cup flour
¼ tsp. MSG

Wash tongues in cold water (thaw first if tongues are frozen). Drain and place on a large platter. Sprinkle the tongues with salt, pepper, MSG, and onions. Put tongues in a plastic bag with about one cup of flour and shake until the tongues are coated with flour.

In a large frying pan render out six slices of fat back pork and then put the tongues in the pan and fry at a medium heat for five minutes. Turn the tongues, cook for another ten minutes and turn the tongues again, then cook for a further ten minutes. Serve immediately from the pan with choice of vegetables.

Townie Fish Chowder

2 tbsp. butter
⅓ cup onions
2 cups diced potato
1 cup carrots
1 cup celery
3 cups water
2 tsp. salt
⅛ tsp. pepper
¼ tsp. MSG
Pinch sugar
1 lb. cod or sole
1 tin mushroom soup
6 oz. tin condensed evaporated milk

Place first ten ingredients in pot. Boil gently until cooked. Add chopped fish. Simmer 10 minutes or until fish is cooked. Add soup. Next milk. Re-heat, but DO NOT BOIL.

Shrimp, mussels or crab, may be added if preferred.

Cod Au Gratin

1-2 lbs. cod fish
1/4 cup butter
1/4 cup flour
salt & pepper to taste
1 1/2 cups (heated) milk
dash worchestershire sauce
mustard to taste
2 cups shredded cheddar

Gently poach cod in salted water (about 1 cup). Cook until fish flakes easily with a fork. Drain reserving liquid (fish stock).

In saucepan melt butter. Stir in flour. Gradually whisk in milk and reserved fish stock. Cook gently until thickened. Add Worchestershire sauce and mustard. Stir in cheese until melted. Add layers of fish and sauce into a casserole. Sprinkle top with buttered bread crumbs. Bake at 325°F until top is a golden brown.

Barbecued Salmon

Season fresh salmon with salt, pepper, and dots of butter. Double wrap salmon or individual steaks with heavy weight aluminum foil. Barbecue for approximately 15 to 20 minutes on each side. Turn carefully without tearing foil so that salmon continues to cook in its own juice. Check for doneness until fish flakes.

If you have the type of barbecue with a cover there is no need to turn salmon as it will be nice and tender.

Pan Fried Cod

Rinse fish in cold water. Pat dry. Dust lightly with seasoned flour. Dip in beaten egg then in cracker crumbs or crumbled rusks. Fry in pre-heated pan with a little low fat oil for 3-4 minutes each side (or ten minutes per inch of thickness).

Salmon-Salad Loaf

1 - 3 oz. pkg. lemon-flavoured gelatin
1 cup boiling water
½ cup cold water
3 tbsp. vinegar
½ cup mayonnaise
¼ tsp. salt
1 - 16 oz. can or 2 cups salmon, drained and coarsely flaked
1 cup diced celery
¼ cup snipped parsley
2 tbsp. finely chopped onion

Dissolve gelatin in boiling water. Add cold water, vinegar, mayonnaise and salt. Beat well; chill till partially set. Beat till fluffy; fold in salmon, celery, parsley. Add onion. Pour into a loaf dish. Chill till set; unmould. Makes 6 servings.

Lobsters

When purchasing lobster make sure the lobster is alive. Choose those that are heaviest for their size. Be certain that they are good and active, this proves that they have not been out of the sea very long. Lobsters which are light in weight for their size are usually in poor condition and watery.

The heavier the lobster the better it's condition.

Medium sized lobsters are best.

Lobsters may be purchased both live and cooked in the shell. A lobster heavy for its bulk will yield more meat than a light one.

Live lobsters should be active.

When purchasing a lobster that has been cooked in the shell, test it by straightening out the tail.

If the tail springs back into a curled position, the lobster was alive and healthy when cooked.

Boiling Lobsters

Sea water is best. If not add salt to a large pot of boiling water. Quickly immerse live lobsters head first into the boiling water. Be sure lobsters are covered. Cook about 10-12 minutes per lb. Remove and let rest on a large platter for about 5 minutes before serving.

Twillingate Lobster Supreme

1-2 lbs. cooked lobster (cut in chunks)
½ cup water
½ cup dry white wine
1 stalk celery, cut up
2 green onions, sliced
2 sprigs parsley
¼ tsp. thyme
½ tsp. salt
3 tbsp. melted butter or margarine
2 green onions, sliced
¼ cup mushrooms
2 tbsp. flour
½ cup light cream
1 egg yolk
1 tsp. lemon juice
¼ cup bread crumbs
2 tbsp. grated cheese

In a large saucepan combine water, wine, onions, celery, parsley, thyme and salt. Bring to a gentle boil and simmer for 5 minutes. Strain and reserve broth. In heavy skillet heat butter and sauté green onions and mushrooms. Blend in flour and gradually add ¾ cup of the reserved broth. Stir until thickened. Mix the cream with egg yolk and whisk into sauce. Add lemon juice. Fold gently into lobster.

Spoon into 4 greased scallop shells or in a greased casserole. Sprinkle with breadcrumbs and cheese.

Bake in a pre-heated 450°F oven for approx. 10 minutes or until nicely browned on top.

How to Cook Mussels

Mussels may be served as an appetizer or main course, prepared steamed or baked. Fresh live mussels should have a beard attached and be tightly closed or close when lightly tapped. **Discard** any that are cracked or do not close. Fresh mussel meat is a cream to a reddish orange in color. To clean – scrub shells with a stiff brush under running water. You may use a scissors to remove beard.

TO STEAM:

Use 1/2 inch of water (sea water is best) or a spicy broth, placed in a deep heavy pot, add mussels (about 3-4 dozen). Cover tightly and cook for approximately 5-8 minutes, shaking pot periodically to cook mussels evenly. DO NOT OVERCOOK!

Remove (as soon as shells open) with a slotted spoon to a large platter. Garnish with fresh parsley and lemon slices. Serve with melted garlic butter, tossed salad and french bread.

TO BAKE:

Place clean mussels in a large roasting pan which has been brushed with some olive oil. Bake at 450° F until shells open (approx. 5-8 min.). Serve with garlic butter if desired.

Store mussels in refrigerator uncovered for up to two days.

Crab Casserole

1 lb. fresh or frozen crab (thawed and drained)
3½ tablespoons butter
½ green pepper, sliced
¼ cup finely chopped onion
2 cups cooked rice
1 cup grated sharp cheese
2 hard cooked eggs (sliced)
1½ tablespoons all-purpose flour
1½ cups milk
1½ tablespoons salad dressing
¾ teaspoon salt
⅛ teaspoon pepper
½ cup dry breadcrumbs

In a heavy saucepan, melt 1 tablespoon butter and sauté green pepper and onion until soft. Place rice in a 2-quart casserole and layer as follows: half the crab, cheese, egg slices, remaining crab, green pepper and onion.

To prepare sauce, melt 1½ tablespoons butter. Blend in flour, then milk. Cook and stir over low heat. Stir in mayonnaise, salt and pepper.

Pour sauce over casserole ingredients, sprinkle with breadcrumbs and dot with remaining 1 tablespoon butter. Bake at 350° F for 30 to 40 minutes. Makes 6 servings.

Dish may be prepared in advance and refrigerated until ready to use.

Soups and Salads

Newfoundland Split Pea Soup

1 large ham bone OR
1 lb. salt beef (cut in cubes)
2 quarts water
1 pkg. yellow split peas
(approx. 2 cups)
1 large onion (chopped)
1 large carrot
1 medium turnip
1 small parsnip
¼ cup celery
dash pepper

Let salt beef soak in cold water overnight. Discard water. Place beef and peas in soup pot and cover with approx. 2 quarts of water. Add onion. Boil gently for 1½ hours. Then add remaining cut up vegetables. Let simmer for another ½ hour or until vegetables are done.

During the last 10-12 minutes add dumplings. Recipe follows:

2½ cups all purpose flour
3 tsp. baking powser
1 tbsp. butter
1 tsp. salt
dash parsley flakes
1 cup milk

Combine dry ingredients. Cut in butter. Add milk. Mix until a smooth dough is formed. Pinch off small pieces and drop in boiling soup. Cover tightly and cook for 10-12 minutes. Do not remove cover while dumplings are cooking.

Easy Dumplings

(DELICIOUS!)

1 cup flour
3 tsp. baking powder
½ tsp. salt
1½ tbsp. cooking oil
⅔ cup water

Mix flour, baking powder, and salt in a bowl. Make a well in dry ingredients. Combine water and oil, and pour into well. Mix lightly and drop by tablespoonfuls into simmering soup. Put cover on tight and cook for 15 minutes without raising cover. Then remove dumplings immediately. Makes about 10 light dumplings.

Newfoundland Rabbit Soup

1 brace of rabbits (cleaned and cut up)
small piece of salt meat (soaked overnight)
1 onion, chopped
1-2 carrots, diced
1 turnip, diced
1 parsnip, diced
¼ cup rice
1 tbsp. barley

In a large soup pot place rabbit and cubed salt beef. Cover with water. Bring to a boil. Pour off this water and add about three quarts more. Bring to a boil and let simmer for approx. 1½ hours. Add diced vegetables and season to taste.

Continue cooking until vegetables are done.

Fresh Meat Soup

2-3 lbs. beef soup bones (may substitute stewing beef)
3 large carrots, diced
1 large onion, chopped
1 med. turnip, diced
1 small parsnip, diced
1 sm. tin tomatoes
1 tbsp. barley
1 tbsp. rice
salt and pepper to taste

Cover soup bones or stewing meat with water. Cook until tender. Add vegetables, barley, rice and seasonings. Simmer gently until fork tender (approximately 1¼ hours total time).

Grandpa's advice on making homemade soup was "Never put potatoes in soup".

Delicoius Vegetable Soup

Great for dieters!

2 large tins tomatoes
1 lg. tin wax beans and juice
1 lg. tin green beans and juice
1 tin mushroom pieces and juice
½ cup chopped celery
½ cup chopped onion
seasonings to taste

Place in a large pot and bring to a slow boil. Simmer for approximately 20 minutes. This soup freezes well. Also you may substitute above vegetables for any other of your choice.

Lobster Salad

1 cooked lobster (cut into serving pieces)
¼ cup finely chopped onion
½ cup finely chopped celery
1 tbsp. chopped green pepper
1 tbsp. chopped parsley
½ tsp. tarragon
1 cup mayonnaise
salt and pepper to taste
1 tsp. lemon juice
leaf lettuce

Place above ingredients in a bowl and blend well. Serve on a bed of leaf lettuce with tomato and hard boiled egg slices.

Serves 4.

Hilda's Macaroni Salad

2 cups cooked macaroni
1½ cups cubed ham
1 cup cubed cheddar cheese
½ cup chopped celery
⅓ cup green pepper
¼ cup chopped onion
¼ cup relish
½ cup salad dressing
1 tablespoon prepared mustard
¼ teaspoon salt

Combine macaroni, ham, cheese and vegetables in a large salad bowl. Combine remaining ingredients and fold into the macaroni mixture. Chill before serving.

Homestyle Potato Salad

12 potatoes
1 finely minced onion
5 tbsp. salad dressing
1 tbsp. relish
½ cup mixed vegetables (optional)
4 hard boiled eggs
paprika for garnish
lettuce

Cook potatoes. Drain and mash. While still warm add minced onion and salad dressing. Fold in pickled relish and vegetables. Line a large salad bowl with lettuce. Spoon in the potato salad. Peel eggs and cut in half. Press at intervals into top of salad. Sprinkle with paprika.

Rosemary's Spinach Salad

½ pkg. fresh spinach (more if desired)
½ head of lettuce
1 can sliced water chestnuts
1 can bean sprouts
5 strips crisp bacon (crumbled)
2 hard boiled eggs (sliced)

Combine all together in large salad bowl. Pour over the following dressing:

1 cup corn oil
1 onion (finely diced)
2 tsp. worchestershire sauce
½ cup catsup
1 cup liquid honey
½ cup white vinegar

Mix together. For perfect results place ingredients in a bottle or jar and shake well. When ready to serve pour over salad. Top with chow mein noodles.

This salad and dressing can be made well ahead of time and stored separately until ready to use.

Delicious!

Favourite Pineapple Coleslaw

2 cups grated cabbage
½ cup grated carrot
1 can crushed pineapple (well drained)
1 cup salad dressing
¼ cup white vinegar
¼ cup granulated sugar

Mix salad dressing, vinegar and sugar together. Combine cabbage, carrots and pineapple. Add to the dressing. Mix well.

Favourite Three Bean Salad

3 med. tins beans (drained) (kidney, yellow wax & green)
½ cup sugar
½ cup salad oil
½ cup white vinegar
1 tsp. salt
½ tsp. dry mustard
½ tsp. tarragon
½ tsp. basil
2 tbsp. parsley
onion rings

Combine all except onion rings. Let stand overnight or several hours. Drain off liquid. Serve in lettuce-lined salad bowl or individually on leaf of lettuce. Top with onion rings.

Will keep for a week or more in refrigerator. Keep covered.

Mom's Homemade Bread

(makes 4 large loaves)

1 cup warm water **1 pkg. yeast**
2 tsp. sugar or honey

Dissolve sugar in warm water (very important that the water is **warm** not hot or it will kill the yeast). Sprinkle yeast over top of warm water. Keep in a warm place for 10 minutes (yeast should be foamy). Meanwhile prepare the following:

Place in a large warm mixing bowl
1 cup hot water **1/4 cup sugar**
2 1/2 cups of warm milk **4 tsp. salt**
1/4 cup shortening or vegetable oil

Stir until sugar is dissolved and shortening melts. When yeast is ready stir well with a fork. Pour into warm liquids. Combine well. Gradually stir in 10-12 cups of flour. Mix until dough comes away from sides of bowl. Remove to a lightly floured surface and knead until light and NOT STICKY, adding more flour as needed.

Shape into a smooth ball and place in a lightly greased bowl in a warm area. (eg. oven). Let rise until double in bulk, 1-1½ hrs. Punch down and divide into four smooth balls. Let rest covered with a tea towel for 15 minutes. Shape into loaves and put in lightly greased warm bread pans. Let rise again until double about 1 hr. Bake in a 400 degree F oven for 15 minutes. Immediately reduce heat to 375 degrees F and bake another 20-25 minutes or until golden brown and loaf sounds hollow when tapped on the bottom.

Butter tops lightly with melted butter and turn out at once on wire racks.

Toutons

When we were children, we would anxiously look forward to the day when mom would bake bread. Then we could sample and enjoy these fulfilling treats: made by pinching off pieces of the prepared bread dough, forming into patties and placing on a hot buttered fry pan, cooked on both sides to a golden brown and served hot – smothered with butter and molasses. Some good!

Homestyle Sweet Bread

2 pkgs. yeast
1 cup lukewarm water
2 tsp. sugar
3 cups lukewarm water
1 cup molasses
3 tbsp. melted margarine
12 cups flour
6 tbsp. brown sugar
4 tsp. salt
3 cups raisins
spices if desired

Sprinkle yeast over 1 cup lukewarm water to which 2 teaspoons of sugar has been dissolved. Let stand for 10 minutes.

Combine 3 cups lukewarm water, molasses and margarine. Set aside. Combine dry ingredients. Add the raisins. Lay aside. Stir dissolved yeast and add to the molasses mixture. Gradually stir in the flour mixture. Knead for about 10 minutes.

Form into a smooth ball and place in a greased bowl and turn dough over 2 or 3 times to grease the top and to prevent a crust from forming. Cover and place in a warm place and let rise for about 1½ hours or until double in bulk. Punch down and form into loaves. Place in greased pans and let rise again until double. Bake in a 375°F oven for about 1 hour or until loaves give a hollow sound when tapped. Brush tops with melted margarine while still hot. This gives a soft crust.

Tea Buns

2 cups flour
4 teaspoons baking powder
½ teaspoon salt
4 tablespoons margarine
1 cup skim milk

In a large bowl combine dry ingredients. Cut in margarine. Make a well in centre and add milk all at once. Combine lightly. Turn out on floured board. Form into a ball and knead gently for a few minutes. Roll to about ⅛ inch thick. Cut out with a biscuit cutter. Place touching one another on a lightly greased cookie sheet.

Bake in a hot 450° F oven for about 12 minutes. Serve hot with fresh butter.

Old Fashioned Porridge Bread

Pour 3 cups boiling water over 2 cups of rolled oats. Let stand about 20 minutes. Sprinkle 2 pkgs. dry yeast over 1 cup lukewarm water to which 2 tsps. sugar has been added. Let stand 10 minutes. Stir briskly with fork. Add to the partially cooled oat mixture:

¾ cup light molasses
4 tsp. salt
¼ cup melted margarine

Cool to lukewarm. Add yeast to rolled oat mixture.

Beat in about six to seven cups flour. Mixture should not be too stiff. Knead dough, let rise in warm place until double in bulk. Knead again. Place in bread pans. Let rise again about 1 hour. Bake at 400 degrees for 30 to 35 minutes.

Nutritious!

Uncle Ned's Cheesy Whole Wheat Bread

Truly different!

1½ cups beer
⅔ cup warm water
½ cup corn oil
1½ cups whole wheat flour
4½-5 cups all purpose flour
½ cup granulated sugar
¼ cup wheat germ
2 tsp. salt
1 pkg. yeast
1 egg, beaten
2 cups cheddar cheese cut in small cubes

Dissolve yeast in warm water. Place in a warm place for 10 minutes. Meanwhile in large saucepan warm beer. Pour into large bowl. Add stirred yeast, oil, whole wheat flour and sugar, wheat germ, salt and egg. Beat for approximately two minutes with mixer. Stir in remaining flour by hand. Knead for about 5 minutes on a lightly floured surface. Place in a greased bowl and let rise in a warm place until double in bulk (about 1 hour). Meanwhile, line two loaf pans with foil. Grease well. Punch down risen dough. On a lightly floured bread board work cheese cubes into dough a little at a time, until evenly distributed. Shape into two loaves, covering cheese cubes as much as possible. Place into pans, let rise until doubled.

Place in a 350° oven for 40-55 minutes or until done. Remove immediately from pans and cool.

Truly delicious.

Paddy O'Brien's Irish Soda Bread

4 cups all-purpose flour
1 tsp. salt
3 tsp. baking powder
1 tsp. baking soda
¼ cup sugar
¼ cup butter
1 egg, room temperature
1¾ cups sour milk
1½ cups currants (optional)

In a large bowl, combine dry ingredients. Cut in the butter with a pastry blender or work it in with your fingers. Mix the egg and sour milk together and then add this mixture to the dry ingredients. Stir until well blended. Add the currants and stir the mixture well. Turn out on a floured surface and knead gently for three minutes or until the dough is smooth. Divide the dough into two pieces, shaping each into a round loaf. Place each in a greased 8-inch cake or pie pan, pressing it down until the dough fills the pan. Use a sharp knife to cut a cross ½ inch deep on top of each loaf. Bake in a preheated 375° oven for about 40 minutes or until the bread sounds hollow when you thump bottom. Turn out on a wire rack to cool. Do not cut for about 4 hours; then cut in wedges to serve.

Best Ever Dinner Rolls

2 cups warm milk
¼ cup butter or margarine
1 large egg, slightly beaten
1 tsp. salt
½ cup sugar (less if desired)
7-8 cups all purpose flour
1 pkg. active dry yeast
1 cup warm water
2-3 tsp. sugar

Sprinkle yeast over one cup warm water into which 2-3 tsp. sugar has been dissolved. Let stand for approx. 10 minutes.

Meanwhile heat milk. Remove from stove and pour into a large mixing bowl. Add butter, stirring until melted. Add slightly beaten egg, salt and sugar. Stir until dissolved.

Add softened yeast. Stir until well combined. Add flour gradually.

Knead on a lightly floured board for 5-10 minutes. Let rise until double in bulk (approx. 1¼ hrs.) Punch down and shape into rolls. Place in a greased pan, leaving a little space in between each. Let rise again until double.

Place in a pre-heated, 350ºF oven for approximately 30-40 minutes.

Remove and brush tops with butter or margarine.

Serve and enjoy.

P.S. for crispier rolls, do not let them touch in pan. For softer crust place close together. Makes about 5 dozen medium rolls.

Torbay Style Spicy Raisin Gingerbread

½ cup butter
½ cup sugar
1 egg
1 cup molasses
2½ cup all purpose flour
1½ tsp. baking soda
¾ tsp. salt
2 tsp. cinnamon
2 tsp. ginger
½ tsp. nutmeg
1 cup very hot water
1 cup raisins

Cream margarine and sugar. Add egg. Beat until nice and creamy. Add molasses. Beat again. Combine dry ingredients in a bowl. Add alternately with hot water to creamed mixture, beating after each addition. Add raisins.

Turn into a greased 9x9" pan. Bake in preheated 350°F oven for approx. 50 minutes. Let stand in pan for 15 minutes to cool.

Nice served with cream or applesauce.

To make your gingerbread a real conversation piece, try using coffee instead of water in your batter.

Traditional Hot Cross Buns

1 pkg. active dry yeast
1 tsp. sugar
½ cup lukewarm water
¾ cup scalded milk
1 tbsp. sugar
1½ cups all purpose flour
¼ cup butter or margarine
½ cup sugar
1 beaten egg
½ tsp. salt
½ tsp. cinnamon
¼ tsp. cloves
½ cup golden raisins
2¼ cups all purpose flour

Dissolve sugar (1 tsp). in ½ cup lukewarm water. Sprinkle with the yeast. Let stand in warm place for 10 minutes. Meanwhile scald milk and add 1 tbsp. sugar. Cool to lukewarm. Stir the yeast briskly with a fork and add to lukewarm milk. Combine well. Add the 1½ cups flour. Beat until smooth. Cover and let rise until light and bubbly, approx. 45 mins. Keep in a warm place, free of drafts.

Next: Cream butter and sugar. Add to the yeast mixture, together with beaten egg, salt, raisins and spices. Then gradually add the 2¼ cups flour, combining well until the dough is non sticky. Turn out on lightly floured board and knead until smooth. Shape into a smooth ball. Grease top slightly and place in a lightly buttered bowl. Cover and let rise until double (about 1 hour). Punch down again and turn onto a lightly floured board. Divide into two smooth balls. Cover and let rest for 10 minutes.

Pinch off bits of dough and shape into flattened buns. Usually makes 8 or 9 individuals buns from each ball. Place on greased cookie sheets 2'' apart. Cover and let rise until double (about 45 minutes). When risen, brush tops with a mixture of 1 slightly beaten egg white and 1 tbsp. water. Make a cross on the top of each bun by slashing with a sharp knife. Place in a pre-heated 400ºF oven for approx. 15-20 minutes.

When done, remove from oven and drizzle the cross with the following glaze:

Combine: ¾ cup icing sugar, 1 tbsp. hot milk and ¼ tsp. vanilla.

Clare's Raisin Tea Buns

3 cups flour
6 tsp. baking powder
½ cup sugar
pinch salt
1 cup margarine
two eggs beaten
1 cup milk
1 cup raisins

Combine dry ingredients. Cut in margarine. Add raisins. Combine beaten eggs and milk and gradually add to the dry ingredients until a soft dough is formed. Roll out gently and cut with a cutter.

Bake in a pre-heated 425°F oven for 10-15 minutes. Watch closely!

Aunt Maud's Economical Boiled Fruit Cake

½ lb. butter
2 cups brown sugar
2 cups warm water
2 lbs. raisins (or one)
1 lb. currants
1 lb. mixed peel or fruit
1 pkg. cherries
1 tsp. cloves
1 tsp. all spice
1 tsp. cinnamon
3 tbsp. cocoa

Method:
Place above ingredients in large heavy pot. Bring to a boil. Boil for 5 minutes. Simmer for approximately 15 minutes.
When cool add:

3 cups flour
1 tsp. baking powder
1 tsp. baking soda

Bake, 275ºF, for 2½-3 hours.
P.S. I use large tube pan lined with greased brown paper.
Truly moist and delicious.
This cake will keep for months wrapped in foil and placed in refrigerator.
Makes a nice dark Christmas fruit cake.

Peach Fruit Cake

1 cup butter
1½ cup sugar
3 eggs (well beaten)
1 tin peaches (20 oz.)
3 cups raisins
1½ cup cherries
1 cup coconut
3 cups flour
1 tsp. baking powder
½ tsp. salt
2 tsp. vanilla

Cream butter and sugar. Add well-beaten eggs. Blend in the crushed and drained peaches, raisins, cut up cherries; and coconut. Stir, in dry ingredients. Add vanilla. (A little peach juice may be added if the batter seems dry.)
Place in greased and lined angle food pan.
Bake 275º for approximately 3 hours or until cake tester come out clean.

Apricot-Prune Coffee Cake

With a difference!

¾ cup butter or margarine
1½ cups granulated sugar
4 eggs
1½ tsp. vanilla flavouring
1 cup sour cream
3 cups all-purpose flour
1½ tsp. baking powder
¾ tsp. baking soda
¼ tsp. salt
¾ cup dried apricots, chopped
⅔ cup prunes, chopped

STREUSEL MIXTURE:

½ cup light brown sugar (packed)
2 tbsp. butter of margarine
2 tbsp. flour
1 tsp. cinnamon

Combine streusel mixture until it resembles coarse meal. Set aside.

Cream butter. Gradually add sugar and beat until fluffy. Add eggs one at a time, beating well after each addition. Beat until very light and fluffy. Add vanilla.

Combine flour, baking powder, soda and salt. Divide into fourths.

At low speed, add flour (one fourth at a time) alternately with sour cream, to creamed mixture, beginning and ending with flour mixture. Beat just until smooth. Gently fold in coarsely chopped prunes and apricots.

Pour one third of batter into well greased tube pan. Sprinkle with one third of streusel mixture. Repeat twice more.

Bake in 350° oven for approximately 50-60 minutes, or until cake tester inserted in center comes out clean.

Aunt Susie's Blueberry Sour Cream Cake

½ cup granulated sugar
½ cup butter
1 large egg (beaten)
1 tsp. vanilla
1½ cups flour
1½ tsp. baking powder
3 cups fresh or frozen blueberries

Cream butter and sugar. Add egg. Beat well. Add vanilla. Combine flour and baking powder and add to creamed mixture. Press into the bottom of a greased 11" spring form pan. Spread 3 cups blueberries over this.

TOP:

2 cups sour cream
½ cup sugar
1 egg
1 tp. vanilla

Blend well and spread over blueberries.

Bake in a 375°F oven for 60-70 minutes.

When cool remove spring form pan and spread with the following glaze:

1½ cups blueberries
½ cup water
½ cup sugar

Boil together gently for several minutes. Thicken with cornstarch.

This can also be kept separate and served warm over individual servings. Top with cream if you wish.

Everybody's Favourite Carrot Cake

(Truly Moist and Delicious)

2 cups granulated sugar
1½ cups corn oil
4 large eggs (beaten)
2 cups all purpose flour
2 tsp. baking powder
1½ tsp. baking soda
½ tsp. salt
¼ tsp. cinnamon
1 cup chopped walnuts
14 oz. tin crushed pineapple (drained)
2 cups finely grated carrots

Combine oil and sugar. Add well beaten eggs and blend thoroughly. Slowly add dry ingredients, then drained pineapple and carrots. Mix well together. Fold in chopped nuts.

Pour into a greatsed 9 x 13" pan. Bake at 325°F for approximately 1 hour or until tester inserted in centre comes out clean. When completely cool, spread with the following icing:

2 pkgs. (3 oz. each) cream cheese
½ cup (minus 2 tbsp.) soft butter or margarine
1½ tsp. grated orange peel
1 tsp. vanilla
2 cups icing sugar

Beat together until smooth. Spread generously on cooled cake. Garnish with a light sprinkle of grated orange rind.

Geralyn's Cherry Cake

1 cup butter or margarine
1 cup sugar
3 large eggs
½ tsp. almond flavouring
½ tsp. lemon flavouring
3 cups flour
2 tsp. baking powder
½ tsp. salt
½ cup milk
1½ cups chopped cherries

In a large mixing bowl cream butter and sugar. Add eggs, one at a time mixing well after each addition. Add flavourings. Combine dry ingredients and add to the creamed mixture alternately with the milk. Combine thoroughly. Do not overbeat. Fold in the cherries.

Bake in a greased 10 inch tube pan and bake in a 300°F oven for 1½ - 2 hours or until cake tester when inserted into centre comes out clean.

Marg's Blueberry Cheese Cake

BOTTOM LAYER:

1 pkg. graham wafer crumbs
3/4 cup melted butter

Combine and press into a 13x9x2 glass baking dish. Bake 325°F for 10 minutes. Let cool. Set aside.

CHEESE FILLING:

8 oz. pkg. cream cheese
3/4 cup sugar
2 tsp. vanilla
1 pkg. dream whip

Soften cheese, gradually beat in sugar and vanilla. Fold in dream whip.

BLUEBERRY FILLING:

1/2 cup corn starch
1/2 cup sugar
1 cup water
6 cups blueberries

Combine in large saucepan and bring slowly to a boil. Cook gently until bubbly and thick. (Keep stirring.)

Spread half cheese filling carefully over bottom mixture. Then the blueberry filling. Next, the remainder of the cheese filling. Sprinkle top with some graham cracker crumbs (finely crushed).

Place in fridge for a few hours and let set. Cut into individual serving pieces.

Trinity Apple Pan Dowdy

8 large cooking apples
1 cup light molasses
¼ cup water
4 tbsp. soft butter
1 tsp. nutmeg
1 tsp. cinnamon
¼ teaspoon ginger
½ teaspoon salt

Pastry for top of baking dish (usually enough pastry for your standard two crust pie)
whipped cream

Core, peel and thinly slice apples (should measure about 8 cups).
Place in a buttered 9x13'' baking dish. Set aside. Meanwhile in a small bowl combine molasses, water, butter, spices and salt. Pour over the apples.
Cover with the pastry. Flute edges.
Slit pastry in several places to let steam escape.
Bake in 350° oven for 50-60 minutes. Serve warm with whipped cream if desired.

Husband's Fabourite Spice Cake

3 cups all purpose flour
2 cups light brown sugar
1 tsp. baking soda
1 tsp. cinnamon
1 tsp. nutmeg
½ tsp. cloves
pinch salt
1 cup raisins
1 cup currants
3 large eggs
1 cup butter or margarine
1 cup sour milk

Raisins and currants should be lightly floured with some of the flour called for in recipe.

Cream butter and sugar, add eggs one at a time, beating well after each addition. Combine flour, salt, soda and spices together. Add to creamed mixture, alternately with the sour milk. Mix well. Do not overbeat. Fold in floured raisins and currants. Pour into a greased tube pan and bake in a pre-heated 350° oven for 45-60 minutes or when cake tester inserted comes out clean.

Hint: Use a long piece of raw spaghetti or straw for cake testing!

To make sour milk: Add 1 tbsp. vinegar to 1 cup milk.

Shirley's Sloppy Sally

½ box raisins
2 cups water
Boil together 5-10 minutes)

1½ cups sugar
2 tsp. baking soda
1 tsp. allspice
1 tsp. nutmeg
1 tsp. cinnamon
1 tsp. salt
2 cups flour
1 tsp. vanilla
½ cup Crisco oil
2 eggs (beaten)

Mix dry ingredients in a bowl, add Crisco oil and beaten eggs, then add hot raisin mixture. Bake 350° in ungreased pan for 40 to 45 minutes.

You can use a tube pan.

Truly moist and delicious.

Great Grandma's Cocoanut Macaroons

1⅓ cups flaked cocoanut
⅓ cup sugar
3 tbsp. flour
pinch salt
2 large egg whites
½ tsp. vanilla
cherries for garnish
(cut in quarters)

In a large bowl combine cocoanut, sugar flour and salt. Combine egg whites and vanilla, add to dry ingredients and mix well. Drop from a teaspoon onto a lightly greased cookie sheet. Garnish with cherries and bake in a 325°F oven for 20-25 minutes or until edges are golden brown. When done remove from baking sheets at once.

Favourite Chocolate Chip Cookies

1 cup flour
¼ tsp. baking soda
½ tsp. salt
½ cup shortening
½ cup granulated sugar
¼ cup brown sugar
1 egg
1 tsp. vanilla
1 cup chocolate chips

Combine flour, soda and salt in a large bowl. Set aside. Cream shortening and sugars, add egg. Beat until fluffy. Add vanilla. Gradually add flour mixture. Combine well. Gently fold in the chocolate chips.
Drop from teaspoon onto ungreased cookie sheet.
Bake in a pre-heated 350°F oven for 10 - 12 minutes or until done.

Hubby's Favourite Apricot Pastries

2 cups dried apricots
2 cups water
3 cups flour
1 tbsp. sugar
½ tsp. salt
1 cup shortening
½ cup milk
1 pkg. active dry yeast
1 egg, slightly beaten
½ tsp. vanilla

Simmer apricots in water until tender. Cool. Sift together flour, sugar and salt. Cut in shortening until it resembles coarse meal or crumbs.
Scald milk. Cool to warm. Add yeast and let soften. Add egg and vanilla. Add to flour mixture. Mix well.
Divide dough into four equal parts. Roll out to 10" squares. Cut each square into 2½" squares. Place a heaping teaspoon of apricot in centre of each. Pinch two opposite corners together.
Place on greased cookie sheet 2" apart. Let stand 10 minutes.
Bake 350°F, 10-12 minutes. Remove at once from pan. Roll in confectioner's sugar.
Cool on rack.

Aunt Barb's Jam Filled Cookies

1 cup butter
1 egg, beaten
½ cup molasses
2 tsp. baking soda, dissolved in 3 tbsp. boiling water
approx. 2-3 cups flour (enough to make a soft dough)

Cream butter, add egg, molasses and dissolved baking soda. Add flour gradually.
Form into soft dough.
Roll thinly and cut with cookie cutter.
Bake in 350° oven for 10-12 minutes. While still hot spread with jam and place together.

Traditional Raisin Squares

1½ cups all purpose flour
½ tsp. salt
½ tsp. baking soda
½ tsp. baking powder
1 tsp. cream of tartar
½ cup brown sugar
½ cup shortening
1 small egg (beaten)
¼-½ cup skim milk

Combine dry ingredients. Cut in shortening with pastry blender. Combine egg and milk. Add to dry ingredients. Shape into firm ball. Refrigerate until ready to use.

Make filling as follows:

1½ cups raisins
1½ cups warm water
⅛ cup brown sugar
¼ tsp. salt
½ tsp. lemon juice
⅛ tsp. nutmeg
⅛ tsp. allspice
¼ tsp. cinnamon
1 tsp. vinegar

Place in a large saucepan and bring to a boil. Let boil for 5 minutes, stirring occasionally. Reduce heat and blend in ⅛ cup cornstarch mixed to a smooth paste with ¼ cup water.

Cook over medium heat, stirring frequently until mixture thickens. Remove and let cool.

Roll out pastry and line an 8" square pan. Add raisin mixture. Top with remainder of pastry. Brush with milk. Bake in 350° oven for approx. 30 mins.

Mrs. Critch's Cheese Cookies

1 cup flour
½ cup grated cheese
½ cup butter
3 tbsp. milk

Combine until well blended.

Roll very thin. Cut into desired shapes. Place marmalade between and bake in 425° oven or until nicely browned.

Favourite Date Crumbles

1¼ cups all purpose flour
1¼ cups rolled oats
1 tsp. baking soda
1 cup brown sugar
¾ cup butter or margarine

Combine dry ingredients. Cut in butter, mixing well. Press half the mixture in a 9" square greased pan. Set aside.

DATE FILLING

1 pkg. dates
1 cup cold water
2 tbsp. brown sugar

Place in saucepan and cook over medium heat until thickened - mashing dates occasionally with a fork. Let cool.

Spread date filling over crumb mixture. Top with remaining crumbs. Do not flatten the top layer too much.

Bake in 350°F oven for approximately 30 minutes. When cool, cut in squares.

Dad's Cookies

1 cup butter or margarine
1 cup brown sugar
1 egg (well beaten)
1 tsp. vanilla
1 cup flour
1 tsp. allspice
1 tsp. soda
1 tsp. baking powder
¼ tsp. salt
2½ cups rolled oats
¾ cup cocoanut

Cream margarine and sugar together.
Add the well-beaten egg and vanilla.
Sift the flour, spice, soda, baking powder and salt together.
Add the dry ingredients, rolled oats and cocoanut to the creamed mixture and mix well.
Place a teaspoon of this mixture onto an ungreased cookie sheet. Flatten each ball with a fork.
Bake in a moderate oven, 350°F for about 10 minutes.
Makes 6-7 dozen.
Great for after school snacks.

Creamy Chocolate Squares

½ cup butter or margarine
2 tbsp. icing sugar
1 cup all purpose flour

Cream butter, add icing sugar. Blend in flour, mixing well. Spread in a greased 8" square pan. Bake in 350°F oven for about 15 minutes.
Cover with the following mixture.
Cream ½ cup butter or margarine, add ⅔ cup granulated sugar. Beat in 2 large eggs, one at a time. Add 1 tsp. vanilla and 2 squares melted unsweetened chocolate. Mix together until well combined.
Spread over the base.
Cover with whipped cream and refrigerate until set.
Cut in squares.

Dainty Cheese Cookies

1½ cups flour
pinch of salt
small pkg. velveeta cheese
½ cup butter

Cream cheese and butter until creamy. Add flour and mix until mixture is very soft.
Force through cookie press to desired shape. I prefer lady fingers shape.
Bake in hot oven, 400°F, until lightly brown.
While warm spread with marmalade and place together.
Truly delicious!

Gingerbread Cookies

3½ cups flour
1 tsp. baking soda
dash salt
1½ tsp. ginger
1 tsp. cloves
½ cup soft margarine
¾ cup packed brown sugar
1 egg
¾ cup molasses

Combine flour, soda, salt and spices. Set aside. Cream margarine and brown sugar. Add egg and beat until light and fluffy. Blend in molasses. With a spoon gradually add flour mixture. Mix with hands to form a soft dough. Divide dough into thirds and refrigerate for a few hours or overnight. Roll out one part at a time on a lightly floured board. Cut out with a gingerbread doll cookie cutter. Place on lightly greased cookie sheet — 1 inch apart. Bake in a 375° oven for 5-7 minutes or until golden. Watch closely. Remove to wire rack to cool.

Decorate as desired.

Banana Jelly Rolls

(Kids love them, so does Grandma!)

white bread
bananas
peanut butter
raspberry jam or jelly

Trim crusts from bread. Roll with a rolling pin, as thin as possible. Cut banana to fit slice of bread. Spread bread with peanut butter and jam, then roll around banana. Roll up and wrap in wax paper. Place in fridge until ready to serve. Then slice to desired thickness!

Peanut Butter Ice Cream Squares

1¼ cups graham cracker crumbs
¼ cup granulated sugar
6 tbsp. butter or margarine (melted)
1 cup dry-roasted or unsalted peanuts, chopped
½ cup light corn syrup
⅓ cup chunky peanut butter
1 quart vanilla ice cream

In mixing bowl combine crumbs, sugar, and melted butter or margarine. Press onto bottom of 9x9x2-inch baking pan. Place in freezer 30 minutes. Meanwhile, stir together ⅔ cup of the peanuts, the corn syrup, and peanut butter. Stir ice cream to soften. Spoon half of the softened ice cream evenly over chilled crust. Spread corn syrup mixture over this. Carefully spread remaining ice cream over all. Sprinkle with the remaining ⅓ cup chopped peanuts. Cover and freeze till firm. Let stand at room temperature for 10 to 15minutes before serving.

Raisin Oatmeal Cookies

½ cup butter or margarine
½ cup shortening
¾ cup brown sugar (firmly packed)
2 eggs
1 teaspoon vanilla
1½ cups all purpose flour
1 tsp. baking soda
½ tsp. salt
1 tsp. cinnamon
2 cups rolled oats
2 cups raisins

Cream butter, shortening and sugar. Add eggs and vanilla and beat until fluffy.

Combine flour, baking soda, salt and cinnamon. Blend into creamed mixture. Gently fold in rolled oats and raisins.

Drop from teaspoon onto greased cookie sheets.

Bake in 375ºF oven for 10-12 minutes.

Makes approx. 4½ dozen.

Banana Cherry Squares

Graham Wafers
¼ cup sugar
½ cup margarine
½ cup chopped maraschino cherries
¼ cup fine cocoanut
1 large banana (mashed)
1 large egg
1 pkg. dream whip

Line a 8 × 8 inch baking dish with graham wafers. Cream margarine and sugar together until creamy. Add cherries, cocoanut, banana and egg. Combine together well. Gently spread over graham wafers. Place a second layer of graham wafers over this. Prepare dream whip and spread over wafers. Refrigerate until set, then cut into squares.

Nutritious Banana Fritters

Peel and cut bananas in 2" pieces. Dust lightly and evenly with flour. Dip in batter of:

2 eggs
½ cup milk
½ cup flour
1 tbsp. sugar
1½ tsp. baking powder
¼ tsp. salt

Beat until smooth. Dip floured bananas in batter, coating entire surface. Drain off excess.

Fry in preheated deep fat - 375ºF, for 3 to 4 minutes. Turn frequently to brown evenly.

Drain on paper towels. Makes sufficient batter for about 6 bananas.

P.S. Batter may be used for apple slices, pineapple slices or apricot halves.

Partridgeberry Crumbles

1 cup all purpose flour
½ cup brown sugar
1 cup rolled oats
½ cup butter or margarine
1½ cups partridgeberry jam (or you may substitute blueberry)

Combine flour, brown sugar and oats. Cut in butter until resembles coarse meal. Press one half mixture into greased 8" square baking dish. Spread this with partridgeberry jam. Cover with remaining crumbs. Bake 350ºF for 35 minutes or until golden brown.
When cool cut into squares. Serve with a dollop of cream if desired.

Apricot Smooch

1 cup vanilla wafers
½ cup butter
½ cup icing sugar
1 egg
1 tsp. vanilla
3 tins baby apricots
1 pkg. dream whip or cream

Grease a square baking dish. Cover bottom with crushed wafers. Cream ½ cup butter. Add icing sugar, egg and vanilla. Smooth over crumbs with wet spoon. Spread on the apricots. Top with cream. Sprinkle with crumbs. Place in refrigerator until set. When ready cut in squares.

Chocolate Mint Sticks

½ cup margarine
2 - 1 oz. squares unsweetened chocolate
1 cup sugar
2 eggs, beaten
½ tsp. peppermint flavoring
½ cup flour
½ cup sliced almonds

Melt margarine and chocolate in double-boiler over low heat. Remove from heat. Blend in sugar and let cool slightly. Add eggs and flavoring. Mix well. Stir in flour and nuts. Spread in a greased 9" square pan. Bake 350ºF 25-30 minutes. Cool before frosting.

FROSTING:

2 tbsp margarine
1 tbsp. cream
1 cup icing sugar
¼ tsp. peppermint flavouring (or to taste)
1 oz. sq. unsweetened chocolate
1 tbsp. margarine

Blend first two ingredients, add next two. Beat well . Spread over chocolate layer. Chill until firm. Melt chocolate and margarine. Spread over frosting. Chill. Cut into strips ¾"x2¼". Makes about 4 doz. mint sticks.

Mother's Spicy Drop Cookies

(KIDS LOVE THEM!)

½ cup margarine
½ cup sugar
1 large egg
½ cup molasses
2 cups all purpose flour
1 tsp. ginger
½ teaspoon nutmeg
½ teaspoon cloves
¼ teaspoon salt
1 tsp. baking soda, dissolved in ½ cup hot water
½ cup raisins.

Cream margarine and sugar. Add egg and molasses. Combine flour, salt and spices. Add gradually with the hot soda water. Fold in raisins or other chopped fruit, eg. dried apricots, apple or maybe chocolate chips.

Drop from teaspoon onto lightly greased cookie sheets.

Bake in 350°F oven for 10-15 minutes.

Makes approximately 3 dozen cookies.

Lemon Crumbles

2 cups all purpose flour
¾ cup granulated sugar
½ tsp. salt
1 tsp. baking powder
2 cups cocoanut
1 cup butter or margarine
1 pkg. lemon pie filling

In a large mixing bowl mix all the dry ingredients together. Cut in butter blending well into the flour mixture. Spread one half of this in the bottom of a greased 13x9" pan (or 9x9" if you prefer thicker squares). Cover with the prepared lemon filling and top with remaining crumb mixture.

Bake in a 350°F oven for approx. 35 minutes. When cool, cut into squares. Store in refrigerator.

Cranberry Squares

2 cups rolled oats
1 cup brown sugar
1 cup sifted flour
1 tsp. baking powder
¾ cup melted butter
2½ cups cranberry jam or freshly cooked and sweetened cranberries

Combine rolled oats, sugar, flour and baking powder. Add melted butter and mix well. Press half of this mixture over bottom of greased baking pan (about 8x12 inches). Spread with cranberry jam or freshly cooked and sweetened cranberries. Add remaining rolled oat mixture.

Bake at 350°F for 30 minutes. Remove from oven and cut into squares.

P.S. Blueberries may be used instead.

Grandmother's Lemon Meringue Pie

PASTRY (enough for double crust pie):

2 cups all purpose flour
½ tsp. salt
1 cup lard or shortening
3-4 tbsp. ice water

Blend dry ingredients. Cut in lard or shortening with pastry blender until it resembles coarse meal. Gradually add ice water, tossing gently with a fork. Form into ball. Place in fridge for 10-15 minutes.

On lightly floured board roll pastry to an 11" circle. Roll with light strokes from centre. Fold in half and carefully transfer to pie plate. Fold edge of crust under, pressing to make an upright rim. Flute. Pre-heat oven to 425°F. Prick entire surface with a fork. Bake 8-10 minutes or until golden brown. Watch closely. Remove and cool on wire rack.

Make lemon filling as follows:

¼ cup cornstarch
3 tbsp. flour
1¼ cups sugar
¼ tsp. salt
4 egg yolks, slightly beaten
½ cup lemon juice
1 tbsp. grated lemon rind
1 tbsp. margarine

In medium saucepan combine cornstarch, flour, sugar and salt. Gradually add 2 cups water. Stir until smooth. Bring to boil over medium heat, stirring occasionally. Boil for one minute or until shiny and translucent. Quickly add some of this hot mixture into egg yolks. Pour this back into hot mixture. Stir to blend. Return to heat. Cook over low heat for 5 minutes, stirring frequently. Remove and stir in lemon juice, rind and margarine. Pour into cooled pie shell.

Top with meringue as follows:

4 egg whites
¼ tsp. cream of tartar
½ cup sugar

Place egg whites and cream of tartar in medium bowl and beat at medium speed until frothy.

Gradually beat in sugar a little at a time. Beat at high until stiff peaks form. Spread over lemon filling, sealing to edge. Bake in pre-heated, 400°F oven for 5-9 minutes or until meringue is golden brown. Let cool completely on rack for about 2-3 hours. Serves eight.

Bakeapple (Cloudberry)

This berry is found mainly in bogs and moist places and reaches a height of 4 to 10 inches. The leaves, two or three in number are nearly round, slightly five-lobed.

The solitary white flower is followed by a peach coloured fruit which is juicy and pleasant when ripe. They are delicious either fresh, as jam or made into a liqeuer. Considered a delicacy here in the province.

Bakeapple Delight

1-3 oz pk. lemon jello powder
¼ cup granulated sugar
1 cup boiling water
¾ cup cold water
1½ cups whipped cream
1½ cups fresh bakeapples

Dissolve the jello and sugar in the boiling water. Stir in the cold water. Chill until it starts to set.

Meanwhile whip the cream (1 pk. dream whip will do), fold in 1½ cups into thickened jello mixture, along with 1½ cups bakeapples. Pour into mold.

Chill until firm.

Remove from mold and place on serving tray. Garnish with remainder of cream and kiwi fruit if desired.

Bakeapple Cream Puffs

½ cup butter or margarine
1 cup boiling water
1 cup all purpose flour
¼ tsp. salt
4 large eggs

In large saucepan place butter and boiling water, bring to a boil. Add quickly the flour and salt. Beat vigorously until mixture leaves the sides of the pan. Remove from stove and let cool slightly . Add eggs one at a time, beating until smooth after each addition. Beat until glossy. Drop batter from a teaspoon onto greased cookie sheet, swirling the top. Place about 2" apart.

Bake in a pre-heated 375° F oven for about 30 to 40 minutes, or until light and dry. Cool in a draft-free place. Fill with bakeapple jam and cream. Dust with icing sugar.

Best served chilled.

Bakeapple Meringue Pie

3 egg whites
¾ cup sugar
1/8 tsp. cream of tartar
1/8 tsp. salt
½ tsp. vanilla

Beat egg whites until foamy, add cream of tartar, salt, and beat until mixture stands in soft peaks. Add sugar gradually, beating until meringue is glossy. Spread meringue on a well-greased pie plate, in form of pie shell. Put in preheated 400ºF. oven and turn off the heat. Leave in oven for 2 hours and don't open the door. When done wrap in wax paper. Should keep for days. When ready to serve; put ice cream or whipped cream in bottom of shell and bakeapples on top.

Bakeapple Parfait

Put 1 tsp. bakeapples in bottom of a parfait dish. Add ice cream, and 1 tsp. bakeapples, more ice cream and another tsp. bakeapples. On top, pour 1 tbsp. orange liqueur over the ice cream.

Serve in tall parfait glasses.

Rhubarb Pie

Pastry for a 9" pie plate
4 cups chopped rhubarb
1 cup sliced fresh strawberries
1½ cups sugar (or to taste)
⅓ cup flour
⅛ tsp. salt
¾ cup cream

Prepare pastry and line an 9 inch pie plate. Pour in rhubarb and strawberries. Combine remaining ingredients and place over rhubarb.

Bake in a pre-heated 425°F oven for 10 minutes then reduce heat to 350° and cook for 40-50 minutes longer or until rhubarb is fork tender and top is a golden brown.

Serve warm or cold with a dollop of fresh cream.

Candied Apples

Wash and dry five medium-sized apples. Combine in a saucepan: 2 cups sugar, ⅔ cup light corn syrup, 1 cup water, a 2-inch piece stick cinnamon (optional). Stir until dissolved. Bring to a boil. Cook covered for about three minutes until the steam has washed down any crystals that may have formed on the sides of the pan. Uncover and cook, without stirring, nearly to the hard-cracked stage, 290º. Remove cinnamon stick, if used. Add a few drops of red food coloring. After cooking glaze, keep it in a double boiler over low head. Dip in apples on skewers (or sticks). Allow to dry on a piece of foil, upside down. (Great Hallowe'en treat.)

Homestyle Cottage Pudding with Vanilla Sauce

⅓ cup shortening
¾ cup sugar
1 egg
1 tsp. vanilla
1⅓ cups all purpose flour
3 tsp. baking powder
½ tsp. salt
¾ cup skim milk

Cream together shortening and sugar. Add egg and beat until fluffy. Combine the dry ingredients. Add alternately with the milk and vanilla. Mix well.

Pour batter into a slightly greased 8x8" baking dish.

Bake in a 350⁰ oven for 35-40 minutes. Serve warm with following sauce:

VANILLA SAUCE:

¼ cup butter or margarine
½ cup granulated sugar
1 tbsp. flour
1 cup skim milk
1 tsp. vanilla

Melt butter, add sugar and flour. Mix well. Gradually add milk and vanilla and cook slowly until thickened, stirring occasionally.

Double ingredients if desired. Freezes well.

P.S. This sauce cooks in a jiffy in the microwave. Just melt butter in 4 cup micro safe measure. Add sugar and flour. Next milk and vanilla. Cook on high for 2-3 minutes, stirring twice.

Mom's Plain Pudding with "Lassy Sauce"

1 cup all purpose flour
2 tsp. baking powder
¼ tsp. salt
⅛ cup butter or margarine
enough cold water to make a soft dough
pudding cloth

Combine flour, baking powder and salt. Cut in butter until it resembles small peas. Add enough cold water to shape into a ball.

Place in a dampened pudding cloth. Tie top, leaving about an inch of space between pudding and cloth.

Meanwhile place a small plate in bottom of a large saucepan. Cover with about 1½-2" of water to which a little salt has been added. Bring to a rapid boil.

Place pudding on plate in saucepan. Cover. Let simmer for approximately 20-25 minutes. Do not remove cover while boiling. Remove and turn out on a serving platter. Cut in serving slices and top with the following sauce.

LASSY SAUCE:

Place about 1-2 cups of molasses in a pot. Add some butter or margarine (about 1 tablespoon). Add a dash of nutmeg. Boil gently for a few minutes. Serve over pudding.

We always had this after a fish supper on Friday.

Heavenly Dessert

1 angel food cake mix
2 envelopes gelatin
1 cup cold water
1⅓ cups granulated sugar
½ tsp. salt
1 tin frozen orange juice (12 oz., thawed)
mandarine oranges
2 cartons of whipping cream
few green grapes (for garnish)

Prepare cake mix. Cool! Break into small pieces. Set this aside in a large bowl.

Sprinkle gelatin over 1 cup cold water — in saucepan. Place over low heat. Stir until dissolved. Add sugar and salt. Stir until combined. Remove mixture from heat. Stir into orange juice (thawed). Chill until slightly thick.

Meanwhile beat cream until thick, fold into orange mixture. Tint with orange food coloring if desired. Fold this mixture into cake pieces.

Grease a bundt or tube pan with oil. Pack it with mixture. Cover with foil and refrigerate for several hours of overnight.

About 1 hour before serving, loosen dessert from pan, by carefully dipping within 2'' of top in hot water for a few minutes. Do not let water go over top. Unmold onto a decorative plate and top with grapes and mandarine oranges.

This dessert may be made a day or two ahead!

Simply lovely!

P.S. For a welcome change why not use frozen lemonade?

Sue's Jelly Roll Dessert

1 jelly roll (sliced) (lemon or jam filled)
3 eggs (separated)
1½ cups milk
3 tbsp. gelatin
½ cup sugar
1 can crushed pineapple (drained)
juice and rind of 1 lemon
pinch of salt
1 tsp. vanilla

Line loaf pan with jelly roll. Set aside. Drain pineapple. Soak gelatin in ½ cup of the juice. Combine beaten egg yolks, ¼ cup of sugar, salt and milk, in large saucepan. Heat until hot, not boiling. Remove from heat. Stir in gelatin, lemon juice, rind, vanilla and pineapple. Set aside until cool.

Meanwhile beat egg whites until stiff. Gradually add the remaining ¼ cup of sugar.

Fold into pineapple mixture and pour into lined loaf pan.

Place in refrigerator to set. When ready, unmold on serving tray and spread with cream. Decorate with cherries or mandarine oranges.

Very attractive dessert.

For variety, next time try fruit cocktail in place of pineapple.

Blueberry Ice Cream Roll

Served with a superb sauce!

3 large eggs
1 cup granulated sugar
⅓ cup water
1 tsp. vanilla extract
1 cup all purpose flour
1 tsp. baking powder
dash of salt
1 pint blueberry ice cream

In a large mixing bowl, beat eggs until very thick and fluffy. Add sugar gradually, beating well after each addition. Add water and vanilla. Mix well. Combine flour, baking powder and salt together. Add gradually to egg mixture and beat until smooth. Pour in prepared jelly roll pan, which has been greased and lined with wax paper. Spread evenly.

Bake in a pre-heated 375ºF oven for approximately 15 minutes or when top springs back when lightly touched in centre. Sprinkle icing sugar on a clean tea towel and turn out cake on the towel, quickly removing the paper and crisp edges. While still warm roll cake and towel up together loosely (from narrow end). Let stand on cake rack until cool. When cool unroll the cake and spread with softened ice-cream (done by placing ice-cream in a chilled bowl and creaming with a wooden spoon). Work quickly so ice cream does not melt. Spread nearly to edge. Roll up cake loosely, wrap in tin foil and place in freezer until shortly before serving time. Cut in thick slices and top with a dollop of blueberry sauce, as follows:

BLUEBERRY SAUCE

⅓ cup sugar
1½ tbsp. cornstarch
⅛ cup water
2 cups blueberries (fresh or frozen)

Combine sugar and cornstarch in a saucepan. Gradually stir in water mixing until smooth. Add blueberries and gently bring to a boil. Reduce heat to low and simmer until clear and thickened, stirring frequently. Cool.

Chocolate Dipped Strawberries

2 squares (2 ounces) semisweet chocolate
1 teaspoon shortening
16 fresh strawberries

In a double boiler melt chocolate and shortening over low heat. Pat strawberries dry. Dip each strawberry into melted chocolate. Place on waxed paper. Chill till chocolate is set. Cover with plastic wrap; chill till serving time (no longer than overnight).

Popular Newfie Snowball

2 sm. pkgs. pineapple jello or 1 large one
2 pkgs. dream whip
sponge cake (cut up)

Set jello, when almost set fold in 1 pkg. dream whip. Place a layer of cake then a layer of jello alternately in large mold, until all used up. When set, unmold on plate and frost with dream whip. Cover with coconut.

Nice!

Jams, Jellies and Preserves

The Native Blueberry

Blueberries are found in bushes rarely growing more than twenty inches high. The branches are green and warty with alternate oblong leaves. The bloom is bell-shaped and tinged with pink.

The berries are blue when ripe with a whitish bloom. They ripen in August or early September and can be used in great many combinations of food. They make excellent jam, jelly or wine.

Blueberry Jam

To 1 gallon berries add 3 lbs. sugar
1 egg cup of vinegar (no water)
Boil 18 minutes at full rolling boil add little butter to keep scum from forming.

Grandma's Secret Rhubarb Jam

6 cups fresh or frozen rhubarb
4 cups sugar
1 tbsp. lemon juice
2 cups fresh raspberries or strawberries or 1 pkg. frozen (12 oz.)
1 - 3 oz. pkg. raspberry or strawberry jello powder

In a large pot place rhubarb, sugar, and lemon juice. Combine and let stand for about 15 minutes or until sugar is moistened. Place on medium heat until boiling. Let boil, uncovered, for 10 minutes, stirring frequently. Add berries. Continue boiling. Boil hard for about 5 minutes or until jam thickens. Be sure to stir frequently. Remove from heat. Add jello powder, stir until dissolved.

Place in hot, sterilized jars. Do not fill to top, leave about ¼-½" head space.

Place in boiling water and process for 5 minutes. Start timing when water begins to boil.

Peach Jam

10 cups finely chopped peaches
10 cups sugar
½ tsp. salt
1 cup maraschino cherries (save any juice)
juice of 1 lemon
juice of 2 medium oranges

Scald and peel peaches, remove pits and chop, then measure and put in large pot; add juices from cherries, oranges and lemon, sugar and salt. Heat, stirring until sugar is dissolved. Boil fairly rapidly stirring often until the syrup will sheet off a clean metal spoon (two thick drops that run together), about 45 minutes. Add chopped cherries, boil up once. Place in hot sterilized jars.

Bakeapple Jam

Prepare berries by washing well. Drain. Weigh berries and to each lb. of berries add about 1½ cups sugar or to taste. Let stand for several hours or overnight. Cook slowly for 20-30 minutes or until jam consistency is obtained. Store into hot sterilized jars.

Raspberry Jam

8 cups fresh raspberries
6 cups sugar

Place berries in large pot. Crush. Add sugar and cook until thick. Pour into hot sterilized mason jars. Seal with paraffin wax.

Rhubarb Jam

1½ lbs Rhubarb (approx. 6 cups)
¼ cup water
⅔ cup sugar (or to taste)

Place in a large saucepan and bring to a slow boil. Cover and reduce heat to simmer. Cook for 5 - 10 minutes, or until jam begins to thicken. Pour into hot sterilized jars.

The Partridgeberry

This plant grows profusely in Newfoundland and Labrador, close to the ground. The oval shiny leaves and bright red berries are easily distinguished. In Labrador they are called Red Berries.

The berries are delicious when cooked with sugar for pies, breads, desserts or as a jam to accompany wild game, chicken or turkey.

Partridgeberry Jam

6 cups partridgeberries
3 cups sugar

Cook berries in a small amount of water (about 2 cups) enough to keep pan from burning. After adding sugar, cook quickly for 15 minutes. Seal in hot sterile jars.

Partridgeberry Jelly

2 cups partridgeberries **sugar**

Cover berries with water and boil for ½ hour. Mash through colander.
Meausure juice and for each cup of juice and a cup of sugar.
Boil until bubbles form. Place a little of the juice on a plate in a cold place. If it jells, it is ready, or if it runs of the spoon in strings it is ready.
Fill up bottles and let set overnight.
Then cover with parafin wax.

Dogberry and Crabapple Jelly

1 qt. dogberries **sugar**
2 doz. crabapples

Cover the berries and apples with water. Boil until soft. Strain. Add sugar, for each cup of juice add ¾ cup sugar. Boil gently until it jells (liquid sheets off the spoon). Cool and pour into hot sterilized jars.

Aunt Irene's Apply Jelly

2 doz. lg. tart juicy apples
sugar
water
lemon juice
red food coloring

Remove stem ends from apples, wash and cut in small pieces. Do not peel. Place in lg. covered pot. Cover apples with cold water. Let simmer for about 15-20 minutes or until soft, crushing with masher while cooking. When done place into a moistened jelly bag or fine cheesecloth and lay in a colander, which is resting over a large container. Let stand until dripping stops. Squeeze jelly bag gently to extract juice — not too much or the jelly will not be so clear. Now measure the juice (should have about 8-cups.) Boil, uncovered for about 3 minutes or until pectin test is positive. Test by placing 1 tsp. juice and 1 tbsp. rubbing alcohol in a small dish. Blend together thoroughly. Let stand for about 30 seconds. If it forms a jelly like mass or clot it's positive if not continue boiling and testing in this matter until the pectin test is positive. Do not taste this mixture as rubbing alcohol is poisonous. When ready add granulated sugar (1 cup of sugar to one cup of juice) to hot juice a little at a time. Boil briskly for about 15 minutes uncovered removing scum as it forms. Test for jelly stage* at this pont. Remove from heat. Remove scum with a metal spoon. Stir a couple of times removing foam in between stirs. Fold in lemon juice and food coloring.

Pour into hot sterilized jelly jars, leaving ½ inch space at top. If storing for long period cover jelly with 1/8 inch of paraffin.

*Test by dipping a large spoon into the syrup. Hold up horizontally. Mixture should run together to form a sheet or using a candy thermometer it should register 219° F.

Makes about 10, small jars.

Wine Jelly

2 cups wine (red or white)
3 cups sugar
½ bottle Certo (fruit pectin)

Mix wine and sugar on top of double boiler. Place over boiling water; stir until sugar is dissolved. Remove from heat; stir in Certo. Pour into sterilized glasses. Cover with ⅛ inch hot paraffin.

Makes about 5 medium sized glasses.

Chill well before serving.

Marmalade

4 cups of sliced fruit

Use all oranges, or oranges and lemons, or oranges, lemons and grapefruit. Cut fruit very thin and add 12 cups of water. Boil down until there are about 7 cups. This takes about 2 hours. Measure and be sure you have 7 cups. Add 12 cups sugar and boil 8 minutes. Pour into hot sterile jars and seal.

Grandma's Sweet Relish

approx. 10 lbs. green tomatoes
5 lbs. onions
4 cups sugar
1 quart vinegar
2 tbsp. salt
2 tbsp. pickling spices (tied in a cloth)

Chop vegetables fine or put through mincer. Add sugar, vinegar, salt, spice bag. Cook until tender. Place in large jar for a few days, leaving in spice bag.

Remove bag and place contents in hot sterilized jars.

Pickled Beets

Wash beets and boil until tender. Place under cold water and remove skins. Slice and put in jars. Boil 2 cups water, 2 cups of vinegar and 1 cup sugar. Pour over beets in jars and seal.

P.S. You will need about 5-6 bunches of beet (approx. 20 medium beet).

Sweet Pickled Onions

2 qts. small white onions
1 qt. vinegar
¼ cup pickling spices
½ cup salt
1 cup sugar

Cover onions with hot water for a few minutes. Drain, then cover with cold water and peel. Cover with water and ½ cup salt and let stand overnight. Drain and rinse in cold running water. Bring sugar and vinegar to boil. Tie spices in bag and add to mixture with onions. Boil 1 min. Pack in jars while hot. Seal immediately.

Colorful Carrot & Cabbage Relish

3 cups cabbage (shredded)
1 cup carrot (grated)
1 onion (grated)
1 green pepper (shredded)
¼ cup sugar
1½ tsp. salt
½ cup vinegar
½ tsp. celery seeds
½ tsp. mustard seeds

In large bowl combine cabbage, carrot, onion and green pepper. Add salt, sugar, vinegar and spices. Combine well. Place in individual glass jars or large mason jar and store in fridge. Will keep crisp for about one week.

Barb's Rhubarb Pickles

2 quarts chopped rhubarb
1 quart chopped onion
1 pint vinegar
2 cups granulated sugar
1 tbls. salt
½ tsp. cloves
1 tsp. allspice
1 tsp. cinnamon
1 tsp. pepper

Cook together slowly until tender about 1 hour.

Never Fail Mustard Pickles

1 pound pickling onions
1 large head cauliflower (2 pounds)
3 large cucumbers
1 sweet red pepper
½ cup salt
1 quart white vinegar
1½ cups granulated sugar
½ cup sifted flour
2 tbsp. dry mustard
1 tbsp. tumeric
½ cup water

Skin the onions and separate the cauliflower into small flowerlets. Cut unpeeled curcumbers and red pepper into wedges. Cover with water; sprinkle with salt and let stand overnight. Boil 10 minutes in water in which it has been soaked. Drain. Heat vinegar and sugar. Make a smooth paste with flour, mustard, tumeric and ½ cup water; add to vinegar and boil until thick. Pour over vegetables while still hot. Seal in hot, sterilized jars.

Aunt Cecily's Simple Tomato Pickles

1 large tin tomatoes
6 apples
5 onions
½ head of cabbage
2 cups brown sugar
1 cup vinegar
1-2 tsp. cinnamon
½ tsp. cloves

Place above in large saucepan and let simmer for approximately 3 hours.

Place immediately in hot sterilized jars. Simply delicious to have on hand when company arrives. Nice served with cold meats and favourite tossed salad.

Homestyle Salad Dressing

1 tsp. mayonnaise
dash oregano
dash black pepper
dash garlic salt
½ tsp. corn oil
a little wine vinegar to liquify

Beat with fork. Mix all together and place in refrigerator until ready to use.

Creamy French Dressing

1 tsp. salt
½ tsp. dry mustard
⅔ tbsp. sugar (or to taste)
3 tbsp. ketchup
½ cup corn oil
¼ cup evaporated milk
3 tbsp. white vinegar

Measure all ingredients except vinegar into bowl and beat until smooth and well blended. Add vinegar all at once and beat until well mixed.

Seafood Sauce

½ cup chili sauce
¼ cup fresh lemon juice
1 tbsp. worchestershire sauce
1 tbsp. white vinegar
⅛ tsp. tabasco sauce
1 tsp. minced onion

Combine all ingredients. Place in covered container. Chill until ready to use. Serve with shrimp, crab or other favourite fish dish.

White Fish Sauce

(great with Salmon)

2 tbsp. butter
2 tbsp. flour
salt & pepper
1 onion (grated)
¼ cup finely chopped green onion

Melt butter. Whisk in flour and seasonings. Add onion. Gradually pour in milk. Cook gently until thickened.

Mom's Homestyle Apple Sauce

3 lbs. apples
water
sugar
lemon juice
cinnamon
vanilla extract (optional)

Wash, core and cut apples into quarters. Place in pot and partly cover with water. Simmer until tender. Remove from heat and put through a food processor or blender, skins and all. Strain. Return the strained apple pulp to pot. Add enough sugar to taste. Simmer for approximately three minutes. Add a little lemon juice and vanilla, if desired. Sprinkle with cinnamon.

Cook gently until mixture thickens a little. Remove from stove and place in desired containers. Serve with your favourite dish.

Barb's Sweet 'n Sour Sauce

1 cup water
½ cup vinegar
4 tbsp. catsup
1 cup sugar
pinch of salt
2 tsp. soya sauce
2 tbsp. corn starch
½ cup water
few drops red food coloring

Bring first six ingredients to a boil. Mix cornstarch with last ½ cup water. Add a little red food coloring. When thickened, add pineapple cubes.

Nice with chicken or meatballs.

I usually double the recipe. Freezes well also!!

Newfie Rum Sauce

(Serve with your favourite pudding!)

2 cups brown sugar
1 tsp. salt
2 tbsp. butter of margarine
2 cups warm water
2 tbsp. screech
or to desired taste

Place in large sauce pan. Bring to a slow boil and thicken with a mixture of cornstarch and water, boil gently until thickened, stirring frequently with a wooden spoon. Serve over cake or pudding.

Spruce Beer Grandpa's Style

Black spruce boughs from young trees
1 quart molasses
water
5 lbs. sugar
1 pkg. yeast

Fill a 5-gallon or slightly larger boiler with broken up spruce boughs. Cover with water and boil for 1 hour. Boughs are boiled sufficiently when the rind peels easily. Pour the water into a container large enough to hold 10 to 12 gallons. Don't strain out the little bits of needles, etc., that may be in the water at this stage. Add enough water, keeping it lukewarm, up to a total of 10 to 12 gallons. The first couple of gallons may be poured first over the boughs remaining in the pot and sloshed around to get all the substance from the boughs before pouring it into the larger container. Then add sugar and molasses, stirring until dissolved. Sprinkle yeast on top — don't stir. Yeast should foam up well on top and depending on size of container may run off the top and down the sides. Otherwise. you may occasionally skim the foam off the top. Let stand in a warm place for about three hours. Then strain through cheese cloth, bottle and cap. Leave in a warm place for a day then store in fridge or cooler and it is ready to drink at any time. Be sure to keep the bottled beer cold or it may explode.

Uncle Ned's Dogberry Wine

8 cups dogberries
12 large apples (chopped)
16 cups water
8 cups granulated sugar

In large pot cook dogberries and apples in the water. Strain. Place in large crock. Add sugar, When lukewarm, add 1 package of dry yeast. Store in warm place until there are no bubbles. Strain and bottle.

Let stand for a couple of months.

Enjoy!

Spiced Crabapples

4 pounds of crabapples
2½ cups of white vinegar
2 cups of water
4 cups of sugar
1 tbsp. of whole cloves
3 cinnamon sticks
1 tsp. of whole ginger

Wash and remove blossom ends of crabapples. Prick each apple several times. Heat vinegar, water and sugar to boiling. Add spices tied loosely in a cheesecloth bag. Cook part of crabapples in syrup for 2 minutes. Remove, add more crabapples and cook; remove; repeat until all crabapples are cooked. Pour syrup with spice bag over crabapples and let stand overnight. Remove spice bag. Pack apples in clean, hot preserve jars. Heat syrup to boiling. Pour over fruit. Process in hot water bath 30 minutes. Makes 4-5 pints.

Uncle Jack's Marinated Herring

Clean and fillet herring. Soak in cold water for a few hours or over-night - depending on saltiness of herring. Skin and cut into small pieces.
Place onion and herring into sterilized mason jars. Pour over the following:

1 large bottle malt vinegar (1 quart)
2 tbsp. pickling spices
water (approximately ¾ cup)
½ cup sugar

Combine in large saucepan. Simmer for about 10 minutes. Let cool before pouring over herring, if poured on hot, the herring will become soft.
Cover tightly and store in a cool place.

Bottled Turr.

Clean the turrs; skin; and cut off back and rib bones where there is not much meat. Pack the legs and breasts in wide mouth mason jars. Add two slices fat pork, one chopped onion and one teaspoon salt to each jar. Fill the jars to one inch of top with boiling water. Screw on tops; loosen slightly.
Process in boiling water for 3 hours.
A quart jar will hold about 2 birds. If small mouth jars are used, the meat will have to be cut in smaller pieces. Do not pack the giblets.
P.S. Pressure cooker may also be used. Reduce time to approx. 1½ hours.

Bottled Salmon

Cut salmon in small pieces. Pack in sterilized jars. Fill jars with boiling salted water (½ tsp. salt). Screw on tops lightly. Place jars in container of water and simmer gently for 3 hours. Screw lids on tight.

"Preserved Moose"

Wash meat and cut in small wedges. Place in jars. Add 2 tsp. salt and boiling water to fill jars to within 1" of top. (Dash of garlic salt may be added.)
Seal jars and then loosen slightly. Process in boiling water for 4 hours or in pressure cooker for 1¾ hours at 10 lbs. pressure. Seal jars immediately.

Dandelion Wine (from Marystown)

Take 3 quarts of dandelion. Pour one gallon of boiling water over them. Let stand overnight. Strain. Add juice of 3 lemons and one orange. Add 3 lbs. sugar and boil 30 minutes. When lukewarm, add 1 package yeast, sprinkled on a piece of toast and float this on the surface. Let stand until all fermentation has ceased and there are no bubbles. Bottle and cork.

Aunt Marg's Dogberry Brandy

Place fresh ripe dogberries (which have been cleaned and washed) in a one gallon bottle. Dissolve 5 cups sugar in one quart of boiling water Pour over berries. Let cool and then cover tightly. Let stand for about 8 days. Then test for sweetness. Add more sugar if needed, dissolving as before. Cover loosely and let stand for about 1 month or longer. Strain and bottle.

Traditional Blueberry Wine

2 qts. blueberries
4 quarts boiling water
sugar
3 cups prunes

Combine berries and boiling water. Let simmer until it begins to boil. Strain and add 6 cups granulated sugar to a gallon of juice. Boil for 5 minutes. Let cool. Then add 3 cups prunes. Place in a crock or jar. Cover with cheesecloth and let stand for about two months, then strain. Pour into bottle and cap.

Lemonade

4-5 large lemons
⅔ cup sugar
6½ cups water
dash of nutmeg (optional)

Cut one lemon into thick slices and place in a large glass jug. Add sugar and press the lemon slices into sugar until covered and dampened. Let stand for 15-20 minutes. Squeeze remaining lemons and add the juice and water to lemon slices in the jug. Stir. Add ice cubes and dash of nutmeg if desired. Stir again.

Conversions and Equivalents

English	Metric
¼ teaspoon	1 ml
½ teaspoon	2 ml
1 teaspoon	5 ml
1 tablespoon	15 ml
2 tablespoons	25 ml
¼ cup	50 ml
⅓ cup	75 ml
½ cup	125 ml
⅔ cup	150 ml
¾ cup	175 ml
1 cup	250 ml
1½ cups	375 ml
2 cups	500 ml
1 pt.	800 ml

1 lb. butter or margarine = 2 cups
2 cups = 1 pint
2¼ cups sugar = 1 lb.
3 med. potatoes = 1 lb.
1 envelope unflavoured gelatin = 1 tablespoon
½ cup = 8 tablespoons

MEASURING DRY INGREDIENTS

Dash = under ⅛ teaspoon
1 tablespoon = 3 teaspoons
¼ cup = 4 tablespoons
⅓ cup = 5 tablespoons + 1 teaspoon
½ cup = 8 tablespoons
1 cup = 16 tablespoons

WEIGHTS
For Fish, Meat, Poultry, and Bulk Fruits and Vegetables

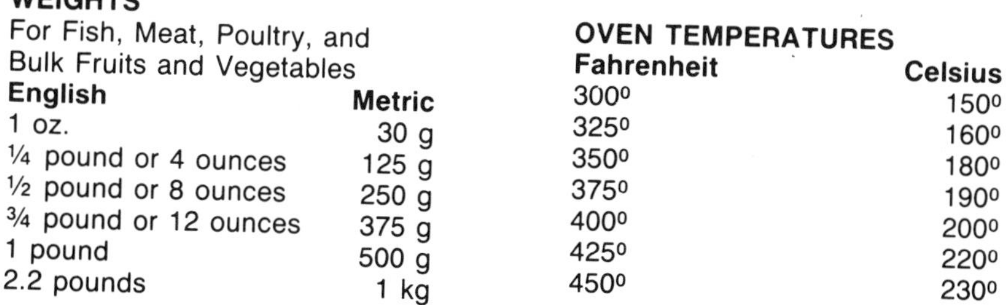

English	Metric
1 oz.	30 g
¼ pound or 4 ounces	125 g
½ pound or 8 ounces	250 g
¾ pound or 12 ounces	375 g
1 pound	500 g
2.2 pounds	1 kg

OVEN TEMPERATURES

Fahrenheit	Celsius
300°	150°
325°	160°
350°	180°
375°	190°
400°	200°
425°	220°
450°	230°

Index

DESSERTS

JAMS, JELLIES AND PRESERVES

Extra copies of

Newfoundland Homestyle and Traditional Recipes

may be ordered from

HILLCREST PUBLISHING
P.O. Box 5492
St. John's, Newfoundland
A1C 5W4

PRINTED BY ROBINSON-BLACKMORE PRINTING & PUBLISHING LTD.